SAMS
Teach Yourself

VISUAL BASIC® 6

Lowell Mauer
with
Loren D. Eidahl
Jeff Perkins
Robert Wasserman

in 10 Minutes

SAMS

A Division of Macmillan Computer Publishing
201 West 103rd St., Indianapolis, Indiana, 46290 USA

SAMS TEACH YOURSELF VISUAL BASIC® 6 IN 10 MINUTES

Copyright © 1999 by Sams Publishing

International Standard Book Number: 0-672-31458-4

Library of Congress Catalog Card Number: 98-87213

Printed in the United States of America

First Printing: February 1999

01   00   99   4   3   2   1

WARNING AND DISCLAIMER

EXECUTIVE EDITOR
Chris Denny

ACQUISITIONS EDITOR
Sharon Cox

DEVELOPMENT EDITOR
Tony Amico

MANAGING EDITOR
Jodi Jensen

PROJECT EDITOR
Tonya Simpson

COPY EDITOR
Christy Parrish

INDEXERS
Mary Gammons
Erika Millen

PROOFREADERS
Mona Brown
Cindy Fields
Eddie Lushbaugh

TECHNICAL EDITORS
Burt Abreu
Jesse Reisman

TEAM COORDINATOR
Carol Ackerman

INTERIOR DESIGN
Gary Adair

COVER DESIGN
Aren Howell

LAYOUT TECHNICIANS
Brandon Allen
Timothy Osborn
Staci Somers
Mark Walchle

CONTENTS

INTRODUCTION

So you want to be a programmer. Great! It is one of the more rewarding jobs available today. Programming means working in the most dynamic industries. Each day new ways of looking at old jobs means that more and more programmers are needed to make them happen. And soon you will be a very vital part of this exciting community.

In this book, you will get a good start into the use of one of the most capable programming tools available. Using Visual Basic you can, literally in a matter of minutes, build a completely functional program. This program can look and feel like the most expensive packages you can buy. And you will have done it with little effort! The best part is that what you will learn along the way will provide you with the knowledge to make yourself a very valuable asset to any company. But if you want to just build programs for your own enjoyment or use, you can do that, too. Programming is that easy today!

So roll up your sleeves and pull the mouse close. In a matter of minutes you will be creating exciting programs!

WHAT IS *SAMS TEACH YOURSELF IN 10 MINUTES*?

The 10 Minute guide series is a new approach to learning computer programs. Instead of trying to cover the entire program, the 10 Minute guide teaches you only about the features of Visual Basic that a beginner is most likely to need.

No matter what your professional demands, *Sams Teach Yourself Visual Basic 6 in 10 Minutes* will help you find and learn the main features of the program and become productive with it quicker. You can learn this wonderfully logical and powerful language in a fraction of the time you would normally spend learning a new language.

CONVENTIONS USED IN THIS BOOK

Each lesson in this book includes step-by-step instructions for performing a specific task. The following icons will help you identify particular types of information:

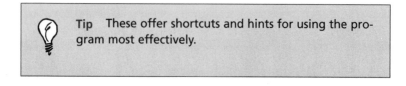

Tip These offer shortcuts and hints for using the program most effectively.

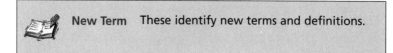

New Term These identify new terms and definitions.

Caution These appear in places where new users often run into trouble.

Specific conventions in this book help you easily find your way around Visual Basic:

- What you type appears in mono.

- What you select appears in **bold, colored type**.

- Menu, Field, and Key names appear with the first letter capitalized.

TRADEMARKS

All terms mentioned in this book that are known to be trademarks or service marks have been appropriately capitalized. Sams Publishing cannot attest to the accuracy of this information. Use of a term in this book should not be regarded as affecting the validity of any trademark or service mark.

TELL US WHAT YOU THINK!

As the reader of this book, *you* are our most important critic and commentator. We value your opinion and want to know what we're doing right, what we could do better, what areas you'd like to see us publish in, and any other words of wisdom you're willing to pass our way.

As the Executive Editor for the Visual Basic Programming team at Macmillan Computer Publishing, I welcome your comments. You can fax, email, or write me directly to let me know what you did or didn't like about this book—as well as what we can do to make our books stronger.

Please note that I cannot help you with technical problems related to the topic of this book, and that due to the high volume of mail I receive, I might not be able to reply to every message.

When you write, please be sure to include this book's title and author as well as your name and phone or fax number. I will carefully review your comments and share them with the author and editors who worked on the book.

Fax: 317-817-7070

Email: vb@mcp.com

Mail: Chris Denny
            Executive Editor
            Programming
            Macmillan Computer Publishing
            201 West 103rd Street
            Indianapolis, IN 46290 USA

LESSON 1

TAKING THE FIRST STEP WITH VISUAL BASIC 6

This lesson shows you how to get started with Visual Basic 6. You will learn how to start the Visual Basic development environment, become acquainted with the Visual Basic IDE, and learn how to use the online Help facility to answer any questions you might have when working with Visual Basic.

STARTING VISUAL BASIC

The first step in using Visual Basic is to install it. If you have not already done this, place the product CD-ROM in your computer's CD-ROM drive and follow the instructions that appear onscreen. After Visual Basic is installed, you can start it by following these steps:

1. Click the **Start** button.

2. Choose **Programs, Microsoft Visual Studio 6.0, Microsoft Visual Basic 6.0**.

After you start Visual Basic, the New Project dialog box shown in Figure 1.1 appears to help you get started. The following options are available:

- **New**—This tab enables you to create a new project or application by choosing from an assortment of templates or wizards.

- **Existing**—This tab enables you to select an existing project by displaying a Windows File Open dialog box.

- **Recent**—This tab lists the Visual Basic projects you have used recently.

- **Don't show this dialog in the future** check box—Selecting this option will prevent this dialog box from being displayed when you start Visual Basic in the future. However, from the **File, New Project** menu option, you will not receive the **Existing** and **Recent** tabs.

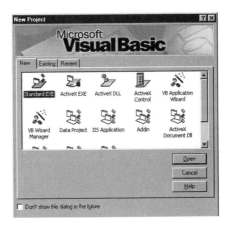

FIGURE **1.1**   The Visual Basic IDE.

Whenever a project is opened or a new project is started, the Visual Basic 6.0 IDE appears. In order to see the different parts of the IDE, create a new standard EXE project by selecting **Standard EXE** in the New Project dialog box. This will open a new project named Project1 (see Figure 1.2). Visual Basic is now waiting for you to start work on this new project.

> **Projects**   Visual Basic uses *projects* to organize the different files that will be used to create your final application. Your application consists of the forms, codes, and controls contained in your project. You'll learn about each of these items in more detail as you continue reading this book.

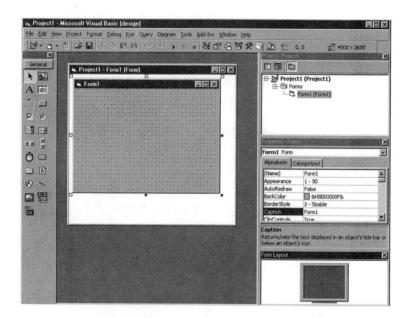

FIGURE 1.2   The Visual Basic Integrated Development Environment
is shared by all members of the Microsoft Visual Studio suite.

INTRODUCING THE IDE

The Visual Basic development environment includes an assortment of
menus, toolbars, windows, and other tools that help you create applications as quickly and easily as possible. This group of tools is collectively
called the integrated development environment (IDE). Although this environment can look complex to a new user of Visual Basic, you don't need
to use all the different tools to write a Visual Basic application. The two
most important features that you will use are the Visual Basic toolbox and
the various toolbars.

THE TOOLBOX

The toolbox (see Figure 1.3) contains the various controls that can be
placed on a form. When you place your mouse cursor over any of the
controls on the toolbar, a pop-up ToolTip will appear, displaying a short
description of the control. You learn how to use these various tools in
Chapter 3, "Creating Your First Application Project."

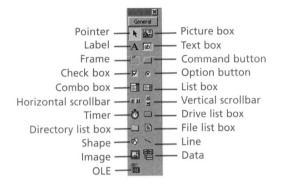

Pointer	Picture box
Label	Text box
Frame	Command button
Check box	Option button
Combo box	List box
Horizontal scrollbar	Vertical scrollbar
Timer	Drive list box
Directory list box	File list box
Shape	Line
Image	Data
OLE	

FIGURE 1.3   The toolbox.

When you start a new project, these controls are already added to the toolbox. However, many more controls come with Visual Basic 6. As you work with Visual Basic, you will learn about more advanced controls and how to add them to your project.

Tip   You can add controls and group them together by right-clicking in the blank space of the toolbox and selecting Add Tab. After naming your tab, you can add a new control by selecting Projects, Components from the menu to list other controls to select and add to your new tab. This helps you organize the controls in your toolbox the way you intend to use them.

CONTROLLING THE APPEARANCE OF THE TOOLBARS

Toolbar   A *toolbar* is a collection of buttons that represent shortcuts to commonly used functions.

The Visual Basic Standard toolbar displays different buttons and changes its appearance as you use the different features of Visual Basic. You can also dock or undock the toolbars, which means you can place them where you'd like them onscreen as you work. Visual Basic has four default toolbars that you can view or hide from the **View, Toolbars** menu selection (see Figure 1.4).

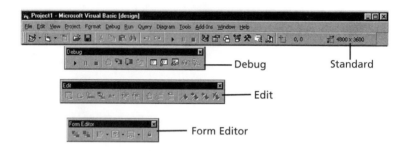

FIGURE **1.4**   Visual Basic's four default toolbars.

The following describes the different toolbars:

- Debug—This toolbar contains items to assist you in finding errors in your code during a debugging session.

- Edit—This toolbar contains items to assist you in editing your Visual Basic code.

- Form Editor—This toolbar assists you in adjusting items on your forms.

- Standard—This is the default toolbar you see under the menu bar at the top of your screen.

WORKING WITH THE IDE WINDOWS

The IDE is really nothing more than a Windows program itself. So, if you can work with the standard Windows elements, such as windows, menus, status bars, and the resizing buttons, you already know much about the IDE.

Most of the Visual Basic windows are dockable and can be resized. If you dock two or more windows together, the combined windows will act as though they are one window and will remain visible if you open any other windows. One of the most important windows you will use is the Form window, which contains your application's forms that you have designed. Don't worry about designing a form yet, just get comfortable with the IDE and its windows.

THE FORM WINDOW

You use the Form window to design the different forms your application will contain. An application can have one or more forms, and each form can have many controls that perform various functions. You can resize the Form window to make your windows whatever size is required. As you resize your form, its new size will be displayed in the rightmost coordinates section of the Standard toolbar.

THE PROPERTIES WINDOW

The Properties window enables you to change one or more properties for the currently selected object. The highlighted object is usually a form or control. You can view the various properties of an object either in alphabetical order or by category. For example, when you place the first text box control on a form, its Name property is set to Text1 by default. You would then use the Properties window to change this property to an appropriate name such as txtCustomer (see Figure 1.5). Most programmers reconfigure their workspaces to make the Properties window larger than the default to speed access to various items in the Properties window.

 Tip   The Name property is listed as (name) in the Properties window so that it is always at the top of the list.

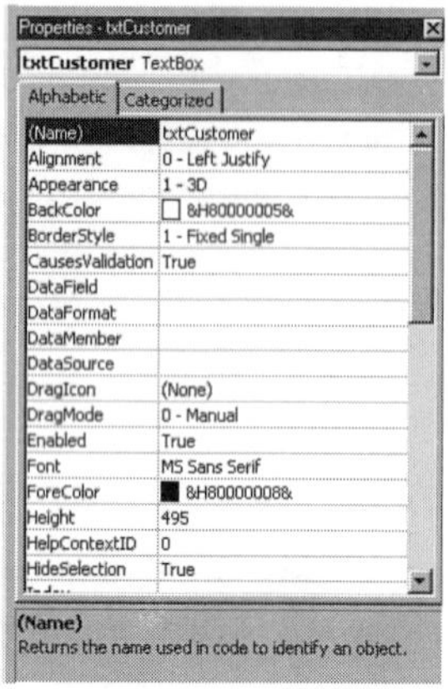

FIGURE 1.5   Modifying the Name property of a text box using the Properties window.

THE PROJECT WINDOW

You use the Project window to manage the various components or files of your project. Related items are listed together in a tree listing. The three buttons on the Project window enable you to display the code or the object (commonly the form), or toggle the folders setting to group or ungroup the related objects. Although the Project window can display the various projects, forms, modules, class modules, user controls, user documents, and property pages for an application, you'll probably be working on only forms and code modules.

THE FORM LAYOUT WINDOW

The Form Layout window enables you to preview the final location on the screen where the form you are working with will appear. If you have an application with multiple forms, using the Form Layout window to align them properly onscreen can be easier than setting their properties by hand.

USING THE ONLINE HELP FACILITIES

The online documentation included with Visual Basic 6 actually contains answers to almost any question you might have while working in Visual Basic. If you are used to Windows-style Help systems, the new Visual Basic 6 Help format will look a little strange.

Microsoft has changed the format of the online help files to match the new MSDN Library format. MSDN stands for Microsoft Developer Network, which includes MSDN CD-ROM subscriptions, an MSDN Web site, technical articles, and newsletters.

You can access the Visual Basic Help system from the **Help** menu by selecting either **Contents, Index**, or **Search** to access MSDN Online. Selecting **Help, Contents** will display the screen presented in Figure 1.6.

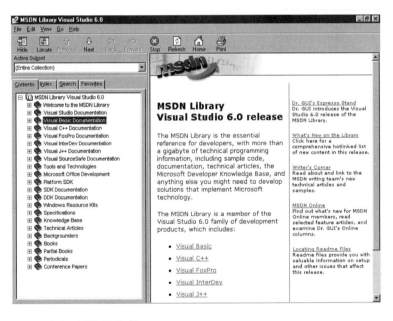

FIGURE 1.6   MSDN Online.

The available tabs offer the following options:

- **Contents**—Enables you to scan Help contents organized in "books" by topic.

- **Index**—Enables you to scan for help through indexed keywords.

- **Search**—Enables you to perform a full text search of the information in the library.

- **Favorites**—Enables you to store links to frequently used topics for easy retrieval.

INTERACTIVE HELP FEATURES

Most traditional help systems wait for you to start the interface and require information on a particular topic or question. Visual Basic includes two very useful help-related features that no longer wait for you:

- Auto List Members

- Auto Quick Info

Auto List Members is a timesaving option that displays a list box which contains the members (properties and methods) that are available in the Code window. Figure 1.7 shows the list of text box members that appeared as soon as the period following txtName was typed in the Visual Basic statement.

FIGURE 1.7   Auto List Members makes it easy to remember the available members of the current object you are working with.

Because Visual Basic "knew" that txtName was a text box, the list contains the properties and methods associated with text box objects. You can then select an item from the list by continuing to type it in or scrolling the list and pressing the spacebar. If you have typed part of the word, you can complete it by pressing the Tab key.

The Auto Quick Info option displays the syntax of any function, subroutine, or method (see Figure 1.8) when you enter the name of that procedure followed by a period, space, or opening parenthesis. The procedure can be either a built-in function or subroutine that is contained in Visual Basic, or it can be one that you've written yourself.

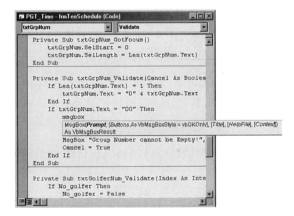

FIGURE 1.8   Auto Quick Info provides the syntax of any procedure without having to look it up in the Help system.

SUMMARY

Well, you made it though the first lesson. You learned how to start Visual Basic and what the different components of the IDE are and how they assist you when creating an application. In addition, you learned how to access the online documentation that comes with Visual Basic. In Lesson 2, you learn what an application really is and how to work with the Visual Basic project that is used to create an application.

LESSON 2
UNDERSTANDING PROJECTS

In this lesson, you'll learn what an application is, how to create and manage Visual Basic projects, and how to add and remove files from a project.

WHAT IS AN APPLICATION?

An *application* is a program or set of programs that performs some useful task. Generally, all the programs that make up an application work against the same body of data or database. In Visual Basic, an application consists of a large number of objects (that is, forms, controls, menus, and so on) and the small sections of code that control these objects. Because Visual Basic enables you to create applications without the need for large amounts of Basic program code, you can create very complex applications that are very easy to use. So, an application is a collection of functions that are combined to perform a particular job in a uniform manner.

Whether the application you are thinking of creating is a small inventory program for the house, a personal phone book, or maybe a day planner, many things go into creating it. If you take a close look at most of the popular software on the market, you can see that many different but related routines create the single, final application.

The application is really a collection of different files that you design and add to a project or folder that you will create. So, to start a new application, you must organize these different files that will eventually make up the application. This organization is a *project*.

WORKING WITH THE PROJECT

Now that you know a little more about what an application is, you will
learn how to start one by creating a new Visual Basic project that contains
the files for the application. A Visual Basic project is simply an organiza-
tional "box" that is used to hold all the different components required by
your application. Besides the standard forms and code files, a project can
also contain resource files, custom controls that you have created, and
documentation files that describe what tasks the application is going to
perform. The first thing you must do when starting a new application is
create a new project that will be associated with the application.

CREATING A NEW PROJECT

There are several ways to create a new project. You will learn how to
build a project from the ground up, and then, in Lesson 19, "Using the
Application Wizard," you will learn how to use the Visual Basic
Application Wizard to create a new application project.

You can create a new project either by selecting **Standard EXE** from the
dialog box that appears when you launch Visual Basic or by selecting
New Project from the **File** menu and then selecting **Standard EXE**.

After you have done this, you have a new project named Project1 that
contains a single, empty form named Form1, as seen in Figure 2.1.

> You might notice that your screen looks a bit different
> than the one in Figure 2.1. This is because I closed the
> Form Layout window and resized the Properties and
> Form windows to suit my preferences. After trying dif-
> ferent settings, you should come to a style that fits
> your individual needs as well.

OPENING AN EXISTING PROJECT

There are numerous ways to open an existing project:

- The last four projects that were opened are available directly
  from the **File** menu.

- To open an existing project not listed on the **File** menu, select
  File, Open Project.

- When starting, Visual Basic presents a dialog box with three tabs
  for **New**, **Existing**, and **Recent** projects.

- From Windows Explorer, you can launch the project by double-
  clicking the .VBP file associated with your project (for example,
  c:\my projects\hello.vbp).

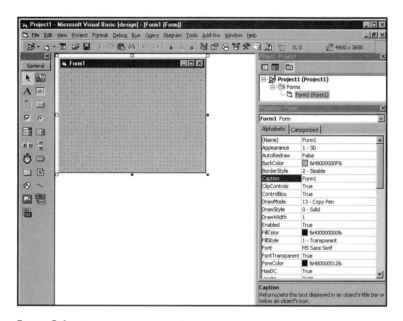

FIGURE 2.1   A new project ready to work on.

ADDING A FILE TO A PROJECT

After opening an existing project, you can add a pre-existing code module, form, or other object to your project. To add an existing code module
to your project, select **Add File** from the **Project** menu. (Note: The **Add
Module** selection adds a new empty module to the project.) Another way
to accomplish this task is by right-clicking the project name in the Project
Control window, as seen in Figure 2.2.

> **Tip** If you cannot see the Project window in your workspace, you can press Ctrl+R to navigate to it.

FIGURE 2.2   Adding a file to your project.

As an example, you are going to add c:\Program Files\Microsoft Visual Studio\VB98\Template\Code\Registry Access.bas. This module includes code that you can use to read and set values in the System Registry from your application. After you've added the module, it will be listed in the Project window under the Modules section, as seen in Figure 2.3.

FIGURE 2.3   The existing code module is added to your project.

After you've added the module to your project, you can reference it within the rest of the project. The following code places the current value of the Windows login in the text box `txtwhoami`:

```
Private Sub cmdwhoami_Click()
txtwhoami.Text = GetKeyValue(HKEY_LOCAL_MACHINE, "Network\
➥Logon\UserName", "")
End Sub
```

REMOVING A FILE FROM YOUR PROJECT

If you no longer require a specific form or code module in your project, you can remove it as easily as you added it. To accomplish this task, select the object to remove (**Registry Access.bas** in this example). You can select **Remove Registry Access.bas** from the **Project** menu or right-click the object in the Project window and select **Remove Registry Access.bas** (see Figure 2.4).

FIGURE **2.4**   The code module is removed from your project.

Now that you've removed the object from your project, you must ensure that you've removed all references to it. For example, if the preceding code sample were still in place and the Registry Access.bas module was no longer a part of the project, the program would not compile. You will receive the error message Sub or Function Not Defined. Note also that although this action of removing the module from the project removes the copy of the module that is used by the project, it does not delete the actual module itself. This module lives on in the file that you added to the project, ready to be used again when needed.

SAVING YOUR PROJECT

At this point, you will normally save your work before proceeding. The first thing you will normally do is create a new folder on your hard drive or server to keep all the components of this project together. After you do this, select **Save Project** from the **File** menu. If you asked the wizard to create any forms for you, you will be prompted to save them to .FRM files. Be sure to save all these files in the new folder you just created. If any code was created, you will be prompted to save it to a .BAS file. You will then be prompted to save your project as *MyProject*.VBP (*MyProject* is the name you provided for the project at the start of the wizard, and .VBP stands for Visual Basic project).

> **The .VBP File**   The .VBP file is a text file that stores information about your project. This includes details that are shown in the Project window, such as which forms and modules belong to this project. The .VBW file stores the current windows' sizes and placement on your workspace. This way, when you reopen your project, your workspace will look the same as when you left it.

WHAT'S IN A PROJECT?

Now that you've seen how to create and modify a project, you should really understand what a project can contain and how Visual Basic handles the project file itself. Every time you save a project, Visual Basic updates the project file (.VBP). A project file contains the same list of files that you see in the Project Explorer window, as well as references to the controls used in the project. Several different types of files can be added to a project. The following sections describe these different types of files and objects.

FORM MODULES

Forms (.FRM) are the visual portions of your application and contain the references and property settings for the controls you have placed on the form. They can also contain the Visual Basic code that you have added to an event for any object on the form, including the form itself.

CLASS MODULES

Class modules (.CLS) are similar to forms, except they are not visible to the user. You can use class modules to create your own objects that include code for methods and properties that are associated with the object you define.

STANDARD MODULES

Standard modules (.BAS) contain all the public- or module-level declarations of constants, variables, and procedures.

RESOURCE FILES

Resource files (.RES) are special text files that contain references to bitmaps, text, or other data that your application uses. The unique thing about these files is that they enable you to change this data without having to recompile the application program.

SUMMARY

In this lesson you learned one of the most important skills you will need when working with Visual Basic. If you do not know how to create and modify a Visual Basic project, you won't be able to accomplish anything in Visual Basic. You learned how to create and name a project and how to add and remove object files to or from your project. In Lesson 3, "Creating Your First Application Project," you'll learn how to create your first Visual Basic project for an application and how to add a few simple controls and some related program code to the form. Finally, you will run the new application to see what you have accomplished.

LESSON 3

CREATING YOUR FIRST APPLICATION PROJECT

In this lesson, you begin to write programs and learn to recognize and use the building blocks Visual Basic uses to construct these programs. Many concepts that you learn in this chapter will be used with every Visual Basic application you will create.

In Lesson 2, you learned how to create and modify a project. You also learned that a project is used to contain all the different objects that will be combined to create the actual application. In this chapter, you use this knowledge to create your first application project. Along the way, you will learn how to place on a form controls that are in the toolbox. You will also add a few lines of program code to activate the form you created so that something will happen when you execute it. Finally, you learn the importance of naming conventions to help you write understandable program code.

STARTING A NEW PROJECT

After you have created a new project as described in Lesson 2, you should modify the name of both the default form and the project itself by performing the following steps:

1. Click the Project folder in the Project Explorer window.

2. Click in the right column of the (Name) row in the Property window to change the (Name) property of the project from `Project1` to `prgFirstApp`.

> **Tip** Some of the concepts covered in this chapter might seem new, and are covered in later chapters. For now, here's a quick guide: As part of your project, a form or module can have specific functions or subroutines that perform specific functions. A subroutine named OpenDatabase can include all the code necessary to open a database required for your program. Wherever your program needs to open the database, you would call the OpenDatabase subroutine.
>
> A *variable* is a storage area named for the information it will hold. The variable Customer_Name would probably be used to save or recall a value that holds a customer's name. You will use these variables throughout your applications; therefore, you should name them in such a way that you'll easily remember them.
>
> If you see other items or code that are unfamiliar to you, check the index to find more information elsewhere in the book.

3. Click on the form shown in the Forms window. This will make the default form the current object.

4. Click in the right column of the Name row in the Property window to change the (Name) property of the default form from Form1 to frmWelcome.

After you rename the form and project, save the project before continuing.

NAMING CONVENTIONS

You might have noticed that the project and form names used earlier in this chapter have prefixes that help describe what type of object the name relates to. By using standard names, you make it easier to understand the functions of all the objects that are used in the project. Table 3.1 lists the standard prefixes that are used to name the different objects in Visual Basic. Don't worry if some of these don't make sense—as you become more experienced in Visual Basic, they will all become clear.

TABLE 3.1   STANDARD OBJECT PREFIXES

OBJECT	PREFIX	EXAMPLE
ActiveDoc	acd	acdWebPage
CheckBox*	chk	chkPickMe
ComboBox*	cbo	cboCustomer
CommandButton*	cmd	cmdCancel
CommandGroup	cmg	cmgSelections
Container	cnt	cntMoverList
Control	ctl	ctlFileList
Custom	<user-defined>	user-defined
Data control	dat	datEmpTable
Data-bound combo box	dbc	dbcCustomer
Data-bound grid	dbg	dbgSales
Data-bound list box	dbl	dblCity
Directory list box	dir	dirFolders
Drive list box	drv	drvDisks
EditBox	edt	edtMemo
File list box	fil	filDisplay
Form*	frm	frmMain
FormSet	frs	frsOrderEntry
Frame	fra	fraOptions

continues

TABLE 3.1 **CONTINUED**

OBJECT	PREFIX	EXAMPLE
Grid	grd	grdSales
Column	grc	grcSalesJan
Header	grh	grhTotalInventory
Horizontal scrollbar	hsb	hsbLeftRight
HyperLink	hpl	hplMyURL
Image*	img	imgIcon
Label*	lbl	lblHelpMessage
Line	lin	linVertical
ListBox*	lst	lstState
Menu	mnu	mnuEdit
OLEBoundControl	olb	olbObject1
OLE	ole	oleObject1
OptionButton*	opt	optSaveAll
OptionGroup	opg	opgType
Page	pag	pagDataUpdate
PageFrame	pgf	pgfLeft
Picture box	pic	picWallPaper
ProjectHook	prj	prjBuildAll
Separator	sep	sepToolSection1
Shape*	shp	shpCircle
Spinner	spn	spnValues
Text box*	txt	txtCustomerName

OBJECT	PREFIX	EXAMPLE
Timer*	tmr	tmrAlarm
Toolbar*	tbr	tbrReport
Vertical scrollbar	vsb	vsbUpDown

Commonly used objects are marked with an asterisk.

By convention, the prefix is always used in lowercase and the first letter of the proper name of the object is capitalized.

ADDING TO THE PROJECT

If you ran the application now, nothing would happen and the form would be empty. The next step in the creation is to add other objects to the form and some program code to activate those objects. In fact, your first application is going to be pretty simple. It will ask you to enter your name and birthdate. Then, when you click the Continue button on the form, it will display your name and age. To do this, add several label, text box, and command button controls to the form.

ADDING CONTROLS TO THE FORM

To add other controls to the form, bring the form you want to modify into focus by selecting it from the Project window. First, adjust the existing form to accommodate the items you want to add to the form.

To adjust the form so that it matches the form in Figure 3.1, follow these steps:

1. Click the form to make it the active object.

2. Grab the bottom middle resizing control. Click and hold the mouse, and drag the bottom of the form down until it reaches coordinates Width-3840 (no change) and Height-3195. This can also be done (simpler) by modifying the Height property in the Property window.

3. Move the **Continue** button down to left-450.69 and top-1347.099 using the technique described in step 2. The only

difference is that you must click the **OK** button to make it the active object before changing the properties.

4. Move the **Quit** button down to left-1971.786 and top-1347.099.

FIGURE 3.1   The Welcome form in action.

ADDING THE LABELS

To add a label to the form, follow these steps:

1. Double-click the icon representing the Label control in the toolbox (see Figure 3.2). This will place a new Label control in the center of the form.

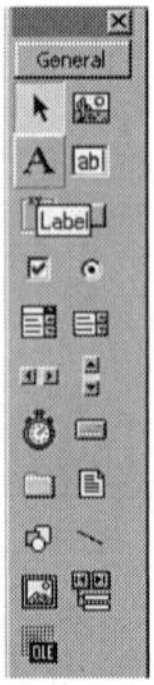

FIGURE 3.2   The Label control.

2. Click the control to select and modify its name to lblName, and press Enter.

3. Change the following properties: Caption-Enter Your &Name:
    (the ampersand tells Visual Basic to underline the N in Name
    and make Ctrl+N a quick key to jump to this field), Height-315,
    Left-120, Top-120, and Width-1335.

4. Repeat this process for the other two labels lblBirthDate and
    lblAnswer, as shown in Figure 3.3.

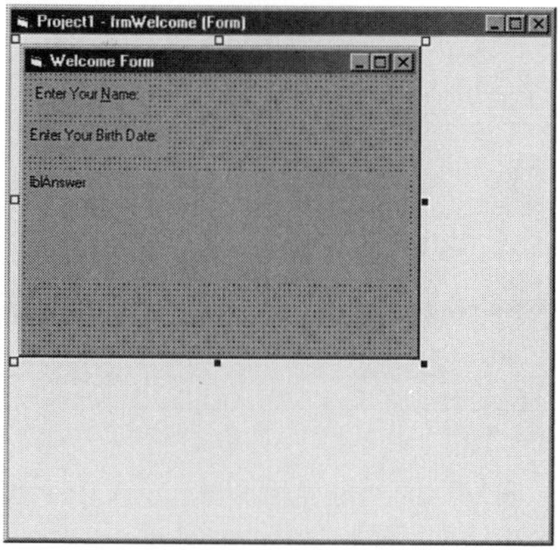

FIGURE 3.3   The form with all the labels added.

ADDING THE TEXT BOXES

To add a text box to your form, follow these steps:

1. Double-click the icon representing the Textbox control in the
    toolbox (see Figure 3.4). This will place a new Textbox control
    in the center of the form.

2. Click the control to select and modify its (name) property to
    txtName.

3. Change the following properties: Height-375, Left-1500, Text-
    Your Name, Top-120, and Width-2775.

FIGURE 3.4   The Textbox control.

> **Note** By setting the Text property to Your Name, you are providing a default value to the txtName object.

4. To add another text box quickly with most of the correct settings required, do the following. With the Name text box-txtName selected, click the **Copy** button and then the **Paste** button. Visual Basic will prompt you as follows: You already have a control named 'txtName'. Do you want to create a control array? By answering **Yes**, you would create a control array. At this time, do not create a control array, so select **No**.

5. Visual Basic automatically named this control Text1 and the control inherited the Text, Height, and other settings. Now you must modify the (name) property to txtBirthDate, Width-1155, Left-1740, and Top-600.

Your Welcome form should now look like Figure 3.5.

FIGURE 3.5   The Welcome form nearing completion.

ADDING THE COMMAND BUTTONS

To add a command button to your form, follow these steps:

1. Double-click the icon representing the Command button control in the toolbox (see Figure 3.6). This will place a new command button in the center of the form.

FIGURE 3.6   The Command button control.

2. Click the control to select it, and modify its (name) property to cmdSayHi.

3. Change the following properties: Caption-Say &Hi (&N was used previously for Enter Your &Name), Height-375, Left-420, Top-2580, and Width-1515.

4. Now the button exists on the form but does nothing. If you were to run the program now, you could click the **Say Hi** button. It would depress, but that would be the extent of its action.

5. Double-click the **Say Hi** button. Visual Basic will bring you to the Code Editor, which will create a cmdSayHi_Click subroutine for you that looks like this:

```
Private Sub cmdSayHi_Click()
End Sub
```

6. You can add code between these two statements to have the **Say Hi** button do whatever you'd like. To have the application calculate the age of the person and display the name and age, you could modify the subroutine to be the following:

```
Private Sub cmdSayHi_Click()
    lblAnswer = "Hello, " & txtName & _
    " You are " & cstr(DateDiff("yyyy", txtBirthDate,
    ➡Now()))
End Sub
```

7. Now when you run the program and click the **Say Hi** button, the label caption changes to display your name and age (see Figure 3.7), just like you asked for!

FIGURE 3.7   The final Welcome form.

SUMMARY

This lesson covered how to create a new application by adding labels, text boxes, and command buttons to the form. Along the way, you also learned how to add code to an object's event to perform a task. In Lesson 4, "Creating and Using Menus," you learn how to add and use menus to the forms in your application.

LESSON 4

CREATING AND USING MENUS

This lesson shows you how to add a simple menu and the related toolbar buttons to a form.

The menu is one of the most important features that you can add to your application. The menu gives the user access to most, if not all, of the features and functions of an application. Even if the application also has a toolbar, those toolbar buttons are really shortcuts to their related menu items. This gives the user a choice when using the features of the appl-ica-tion. Because of the amount of space available on a form, menus generally provide more features than a toolbar can. However, with Visual Basic 6 toolbars can include drop-down menu lists that provide additional options.

Fortunately, Visual Basic enables you to create menus and toolbars with very little programming. By using the tools included with Visual Basic, you can design and create the menu and toolbar quickly and concentrate on the code you need to add to provide the functions you want in the application. This chapter shows you how to add both a simple menu and the related toolbar buttons to a form. After you have completed this chapter, you will be able to add any menu or toolbar item you need for your application pro-cessing.

A BRIEF HISTORY

Although menus are included in every application you see in Windows today, they were not always considered an integral part of an application. Before Windows was widely used, most programs written for a computer used different types of keystrokes to execute a function. As you can guess, at some point, the number of features outnumbered the available keystroke commands. This is when the first menu appeared. By listing the features of a program along the top of the screen, the user was able to select a function using the arrow keys. Then, when Windows was

introduced with the mouse, the arrow keys gave way to the mouse click.
Now, when users want to use a particular function or request some action,
they need only select the appropriate menu item and click on it.

The second helpful feature that was added to an application because of
Windows was the toolbar. Because the toolbar could display only buttons,
all the available toolbar functions were displayed at once. This made it
easier for the user to choose a function without having to remember which
main menu it was in. Together, these two features have made Windows
applications easier and quicker to use. However, until Visual Basic was
introduced, the creation of these features was difficult even for the most
experienced programmer.

ADDING A MENU TO AN APPLICATION

Adding a menu to an application has become a very simple process using
the Visual Basic Menu Editor. The Menu Editor assists you in designing
and creating menus. Not surprisingly, the Menu Editor has remained
unchanged for several years. A menu can appear on any or all the forms
that are used in your application. However, a menu appears in only one
place on a form, at the top. Before actually adding the menu items to your
application, you should analyze your application and determine what
functions you want or need to put on the menu and how to organize these
functions.

To get an idea of the types of organization you can do, look at the menu
for Visual Basic itself (see Figure 4.1). You can see that there are several
groups of functions to choose from. In fact, most applications use a standard set of groupings like the following:

- **File**
- **Edit**
- **View**
- **Format**
- **Tools**
- **Window**
- **Help**

Besides these main groupings, there are usually others that are added specifically for the application. In Visual Basic's case, these are

- **Project**

- **Debug**

- **Run**

- **Add-Ins**

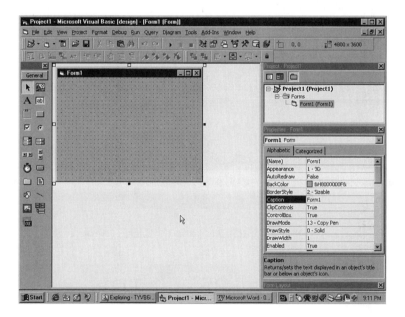

FIGURE **4.1**   Using both standard and customized menu groupings in an application.

STARTING THE MENU EDITOR

To add a menu, you must first display the form you want to add it to. The Menu Editor then creates a menu for that form. To start the Menu Editor (see Figure 4.2), pull down the **Tools** menu and choose **Menu Editor**.

The top half of the Editor, called the Menu Control Properties area, lets you set the properties for a given menu item and the overall menu bar.

The large empty area at the bottom of the editor displays the current menu structure as you create it. Although there are several properties that you can modify for a menu item, there are only two that you must enter for each item.

- Caption—The menu item name that you want the user to see on the menu bar.

- Name—The control name that you assign to each menu item that will be used in the program code.

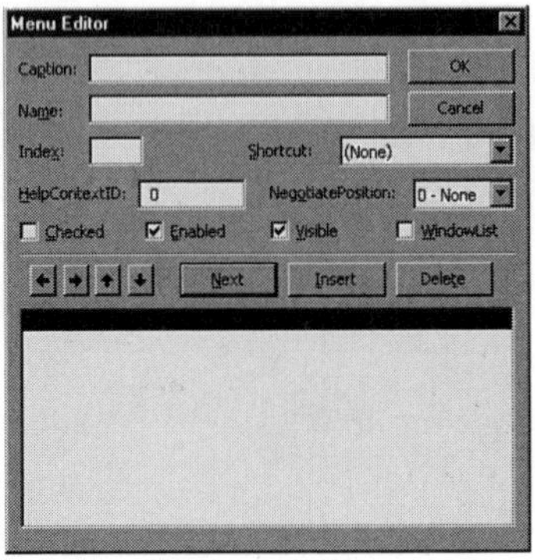

FIGURE 4.2   Creating menu items using the Menu Editor.

> **Tip** When naming the menu items, try to use prefixes that tell you first, that the control is a menu item; second, which group it is in; and finally, what the function of that menu item is. For example, the name mnuFileOpen tells you that the control is a menu item in the File group that will open a file.

For the purposes of this chapter, you can leave the default setting for the remaining properties.

ADDING THE MENU ITEMS

After you know the menu items you want to add, you can start creating the menu itself. For each item you add, enter the caption and name of that

item, and then press Enter to go to the next position in the menu. Add the
menu items listed in Table 4.1 using the Menu Editor but do not close the
editor.

TABLE 4.1   THE MENU ITEMS FOR THE DEMO APPLICATION

CAPTION	NAME
File	mnuFile
Open	mnuFileOpen
Save	mnuFileSave
Exit	mnuFileExit
Edit	mnuEdit
Cut	mnuEditCut
Copy	mnuEditCopy

If you used the menu as is, every item you added would be displayed as a
top-level option, as shown in Figure 4.3.

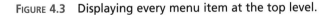

FIGURE 4.3   Displaying every menu item at the top level.

To prevent this, you must specify which items are contained within a
group. To do this, select the menu item in the list at the bottom of the editor and click the right arrow on the editor. This will indent the menu item,
signifying that it is a child of the item above it that is not indented. Figure
4.4 shows the same menu items with the appropriate indentations.

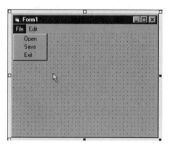

FIGURE 4.4   The final menu items.

INSERTING THE PROGRAM CODE

After you have closed the Menu Editor, the menu is displayed on the form. In fact, it will perform the same in Design mode as in Run mode. This means that you can test the menu by selecting the different items to see whether the drop-down selections are correct. The last step in the process of using a menu is to add the code to the menu item's Click event routine that executes the related process. This can be done using a call to another routine, or you can place the program code directly in the Click routine. To display the Click routine for a given menu item, select it from the menu in Design mode. This will display the Click routine for that item in the Code Editor (see Figure 4.5). At this point you can add the code required.

FIGURE 4.5   Adding the program code required to the menu item's Click event routine.

USING A TOOLBAR

Adding a toolbar to the application is really quite easy if you have already added the menu. The hardest part of adding a toolbar is actually including it on the form and inserting the buttons and images that you want to use. Once again, Visual Basic provides a tool that assists you in this process. By adding the Application Wizard in the **Add-Ins** menu, you also get a Toolbar Wizard that walks you through the steps needed to add a toolbar.

THE TOOLBAR WIZARD

To add the Application Wizard, pull down the **Add-Ins** menu and choose **Add-Ins Manager** (see Figure 4.6). Then double-click the Application Wizard to load it, and click OK to close the Manager.

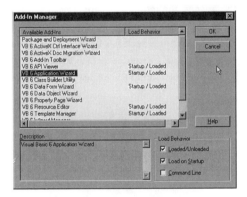

FIGURE **4.6**   Adding the Application Wizard to Visual Basic.

Now, to add a toolbar, pull down the **Add-Ins** menu and choose **Toolbar Wizard**. This will display an Introduction dialog box that you can bypass by clicking the **Next** button.

SELECTING BUTTON IMAGES

The dialog box now shown (see Figure 4.7) displays all the available images that you can use for buttons on the toolbar.

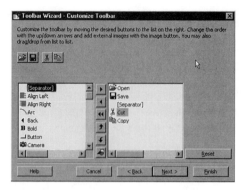

FIGURE 4.7   Selecting the images for the toolbar.

As you select the images, the toolbar you are creating is displayed at the top of the dialog form. Select the images that correspond to the menu items you added in the previous section of this chapter and click the **Finish** button to actually add the toolbar to the form. Figure 4.8 shows the final form with both the menu and toolbar displayed.

FIGURE 4.8   The final form, including the menu and toolbar.

ADDING THE CODE

As with the menu, the final step is to add the code to the toolbar's Click event routine. Even with this, the Toolbar Wizard has helped you. If you double-click on the toolbar, the ButtonClick event will be displayed in the Code Editor (see Figure 4.9). You should see that there is already code placed there by the wizard.

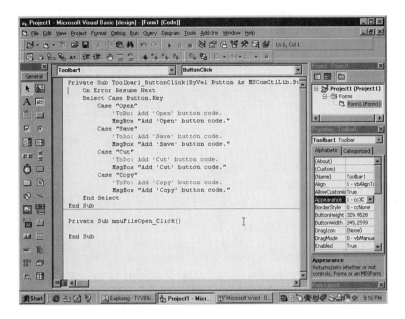

FIGURE 4.9   Adding the program code to the ButtonClick event.

To identify which button was actually selected by the user, the Select statement is used to test the Button.Key value passed to the routine. The Button.Key value contains the Key value that was created by the wizard that relates to that button's functions. All you must do is add the program code to the associated Case statement to execute the application process. For any button that has a corresponding menu item, you need only call that menu item as shown in the following example:

```
Call mnuFileOpen_Click
```

SUMMARY

As you can see, adding both menus and toolbars to your application is really quite simple. Both the Menu Editor and Toolbar Wizard provide you with the tools to create these objects without having to worry about the behind-the-scenes work required for the menu and toolbar processing. All you have to concern yourself with is the code you must add to them. By using these objects in your application, you have provided the user with a quick and easy way to access most of the application's functions and features.

LESSON 5

OTHER BASIC CONTROLS

In Lesson 3, you learned how to use the three most commonly used controls in Visual Basic. In this lesson, you learn how to use the Check Box and Option Button controls to enable users to answer simple questions.

Although option buttons and check boxes are both similar to the Command Button control, making them fully functional in an application requires some additional programming. A check box is like a light switch, it is either on or off. Option buttons work very much the same way because they are either on or off. However, when two or more option buttons are on the same form, only one option button can be on at one time. This is different from check boxes, which allow as many to be selected as needed.

WORKING WITH CHECK BOXES

A check box offers an option for the user. It might appear by itself (see Figure 5.1) or with several other check boxes (see Figure 5.2). The check box, when clicked, will display a check mark (meaning that it is selected) and the check mark will go away if the user clicks the check box again.

As you can see in Figure 5.1, many of the most common Windows applications use check boxes to ask simple Yes/No questions.

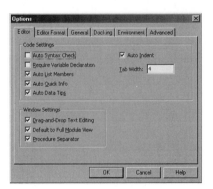

FIGURE 5.1   Using the check box to ask a simple question.

FIGURE 5.2   Using the check box to allow multiple selections by the user.

The check box property that determines the current state of the check box is the Value property. If the Value property is True, the check box is selected and the check mark will appear; but if the Value is False, the check box is not selected and the check box is empty. To check whether or not a check box is selected, you would use the If...End If statement as shown in the following code:

```
If chkQuestion1.Value = True Then
    'Add code here to process the selected checkbox
Else
    'Add code here to process the unselected checkbox
End If
```

CREATING A CHECK BOX

Although the basic check box has been used in almost every Windows application, there is a second type of check box that can be used by simply changing the style of the check box control. The two styles of check boxes are listed as follows:

- Standard check boxes use the familiar box that is either empty or contains a check mark.

- Graphical check boxes look just like a command button. However, when the check box is deselected, the button is up, and when the check box is selected, the button is down.

Figure 5.3 shows the appearance of each of the two check box styles, both selected and deselected.

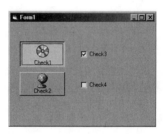

FIGURE 5.3   The graphical check box can add new spice to a boring form.

To create a check box, select the check box control from the toolbox and draw it on your form. When you first place it on the form, its caption contains the default text of Check1, which is also the default name of the control. As with the other controls you have used, you should change both the Name and the Caption properties. As you can see, the Caption property enables you to add a label description to the check box without the need of adding and then aligning a label control to the check box itself.

Changing the Appearance of a Standard Check Box

When using the standard check box style, there are several properties that you can modify to change its appearance.

- Change the font properties for the caption
- Modify both the ForeColor and the BackColor
- Create either a flat or 3D look with the Appearance property
- Choose the side of the box where the caption is to be displayed

Using these properties allows you to customize the look of any form that uses check boxes.

Changing the Appearance of a Graphical Check Box

Unlike the standard check box style, the graphical style provides a few more options that can make it easier on the user to understand the options. Besides the properties already listed for the standard display style, the property that you want to concentrate on for a graphical check box is the Picture property. In fact, when you use pictures, you can specify three different pictures for the check box to use, one for each of the three states that the check box can be in. These states are listed in Table 5.1 and shown in Figure 5.4.

Table 5.1 Indicating the State of the Graphical Check Box

Property	State	Description
DisabledPicture	Disabled	The Enabled property of the control has been set to False. This prevents the user from changing the control's Value property.
DownPicture	Checked	This indicates that the check box has been selected.
Picture	Unchecked	The check box has not been selected.

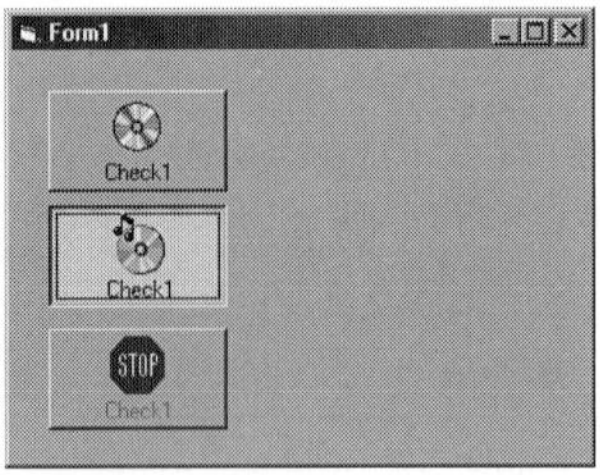

FIGURE 5.4   Indicating the state of the graphical check box.

WORKING WITH OPTION BUTTONS

Besides using check boxes to interact with the user for the selection of options, Visual Basic also comes with the Option Button control. This control lets the user select from one of several choices. However, unlike the check box, the user can select only one option button at a time. This type of interaction is the same as a multiple-choice test. Figure 5.5 shows four option buttons with only one selected. The way this control works, if the user selects another option button, the one that was selected will be deselected, and the new button will be selected.

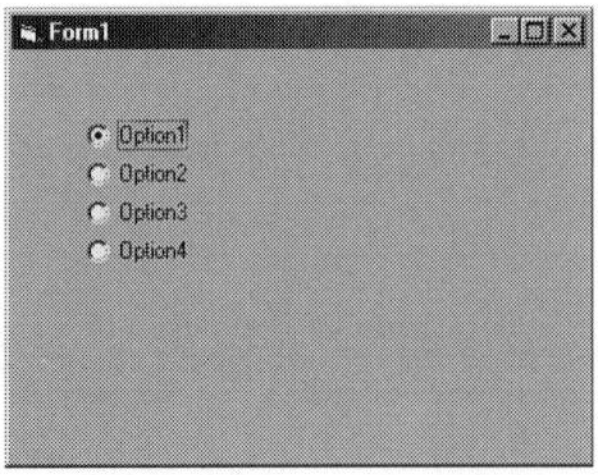

FIGURE 5.5   Selecting one choice from a group.

The nice part about this entire process is that Visual Basic takes care of deselecting the first option button and selecting the new one.

CREATING OPTION BUTTONS

In order to use option buttons, you must add a button for each possible choice the user can select. If the application is asking which credit card is being used, there should be a button for each card as shown in Figure 5.5. Like the check box, you would create a set of option buttons on the form by drawing each button on the form and then setting its properties. In addition, the Caption property of the option button is used to contain the text that is displayed along side the button on the form.

Caution   Although there is no limit to the number of option buttons that can be placed on a form, never place just one option button on the form. If you do that, the user will be able to select that option button, but never deselect it.

Tip   When placing a set of option buttons on a form, you should set the Value property of the default choice to True. This will select that button when the form is loaded.

The option button has the same capabilities as a check box for controlling the appearance of a single option button. The option button can also be displayed as either a standard button or as a graphical button (see Figure 5.6).

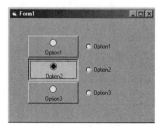

FIGURE 5.6   Choosing the standard or graphical style.

GETTING THE USER'S SELECTION

When your application's code is executing, it will use the Value property of the option button to determine which button has been selected. This is done by checking each option button individually (see Listing 5.1), and then performing the required process for that selection.

LISTING 5.1   TESTING INDIVIDUAL OPTION BUTTONS BY NAME

```
If AMEX.Value Then
    'Process an AMEX Charge
ElseIf MC.Value Then
    'Process an MC Charge
ElseIf VISA.Value Then
    'Process an VISA Charge
EndIf
```

CREATING OPTION BUTTON GROUPS USING FRAMES

Although the user can select only one option button from the set that is displayed on a form, you will probably need to present several different groups of option buttons to the user. However, if you place all the different option buttons directly on the form as shown in Figure 5.7, the user will still be able to select only one.

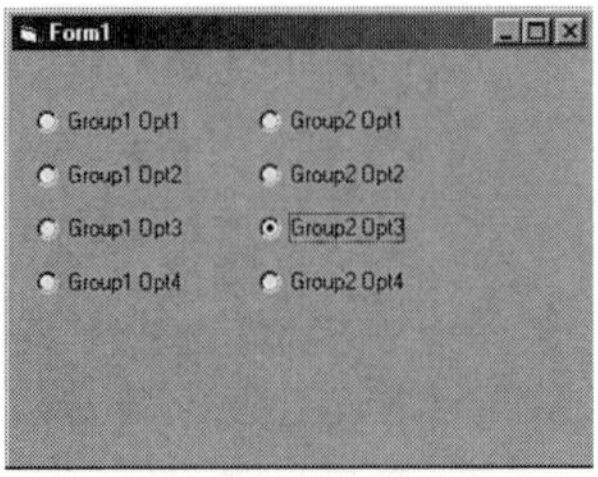

FIGURE 5.7   Multiple option button groups on the same form.

The secret to creating button groups on the same form is to use a container control, which can hold other controls within its frame or border. Visual Basic comes with several container controls that can be used for this purpose, including the following:

- Frame

- Picture

- SSTab

- Shape

Any controls that are placed within a container control will be treated as part of that container. When you add option buttons to a container, they will be treated as a single group of buttons in that container. The most common container control used with option buttons is the Frame control. Figure 5.8 shows the same example as Figure 5.7, but Frame controls are used to group the different sets of option buttons. This allows you to place as many different sets of option buttons on a single form as you need.

FIGURE 5.8   Grouping unique option button groups using frames.

SUMMARY

This lesson has shown you how to use check boxes and option buttons to provide single- and multiple-selection lists to the user with a minimal amount of code. When using these controls to present simple Yes/No or selection questions or choices to the user, you are making the application easier for them to use.

LESSON 6

USING ADVANCED CONTROLS

In this lesson, you'll learn how to add and use list boxes and combo boxes to your form, and how to use the Timer control.

TYPES OF LIST BOXES

Although the simple list box enables you to enter the list items as properties, this is not normally done at design time. Remember that if these are set as properties, when changes must be made you will have to modify the list property in design mode, recompile, and redistribute the application. This is no small task, and could cause other errors.

THE SIMPLE LIST BOX

The simple list box control enables you to display a list from which the user can select one or more items. To add items to the list box control, Visual Basic provides the AddItem method. You probably will initialize the list when the form is initially loaded by using the Form_Load() subroutine. This subroutine executes before the form is actually displayed. However, the code that loads the list can be used anywhere there is a need to add or reset the list. You can use Listing 6.1 to populate a list similar to the one displayed in Figure 6.1.

LISTING 6.1   A SIMPLE LIST BOX WITH A SELECTION

```
Private Sub Form_Load()
    'create and fill the Choice List
lstChoice.AddItem "New York"
lstChoice.AddItem "New Jersey"
lstChoice.AddItem "Washington D.C."
lstChoice.AddItem "Atlanta"
lstChoice.AddItem "Dallas"
lstChoice.AddItem "Cleveland"
lstChoice.AddItem "Chicago"
lstChoice.AddItem "Los Angeles"
lstChoice.AddItem "San Francisco"
End Sub
```

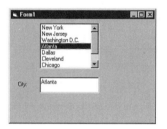

FIGURE 6.1   A simple list box.

A simple list box is presented for the user to select from. You can add code to the list box's Click event routine to take action based on which items are selected.

Notice that the list was displayed as it was added by the code. Visual Basic uses an Index value to reference each item in the list. These are assigned in the order in which the items are added to the list. The index value starts at 0 and increases through the number of items in the list. Two special properties are available to help you use the items in the list. ListCount (for example, lstChoice.ListCount) provides a current count of the items in the list. Therefore, to process through *n* items in a list you would process a loop (see Chapter 12, "Controlling Program Flow") from 0 to n-1. ListIndex (for example, lstChoice.ListIndex) returns the Index value of the currently selected item.

You can remove an item using the RemoveItem method. This method requires knowing the item's Index value. For example, to remove the second item from the list you would use the following statement (remember, the list is zero based):

```
lstChoice.RemoveItem 1
```

If you want to remove all the items in a list, Visual Basic offers the `Clear` method, which is invoked as

```
lstChoice.Clear
```

Now notice how the list appears. The cities are listed in the order in which they were added to the list, not in alphabetical order. Visual Basic offers a simple solution to this task. The list has a property named `Sorted` that when set to `True` causes Visual Basic to reorder the list after each add or remove operation. This means you can add the items to the list in any order, and they will be stored in the list (and onscreen) in proper alphabetical order. Also, notice that if the contents of a list do not properly fit in the list box's list areas, horizontal or vertical scrollbars will appear in the list box.

In order to let the user select more than one item from the list, the control has a `Multi-Select` property that enables your users to press the Ctrl key and select more than one item at a time. In this case, a single text box cannot display the values selected. You would need to determine another method (such as another list box) to display the current selections. This can be determined by looping through the list as shown here:

```
Private Sub Command1_Click ()
    Dim I ' Declare variable.
    ' Clear all items from the list.
    lstSelected.Clear
    ' If an item is selected, add it to the selected list
    For I = 0 To lstChoice.ListCount - 1
        If lstChoice.Selected(I) Then lstSelected.
        ➥AddItem lstChoice.List(I)
        End If
    Next I
End Sub
```

Another method of visually displaying which items in a list are selected is to modify the `Style` property. This property has two settings, `0-Standard`, which displays the list box items only, and `1-Checkbox`, which displays a check box before each item. Its "selected" property is changed when the user clicks the check box.

COMBO BOX CONTROLS

Although the simple list box enables users to make selections from a list, the actual control on the form takes up valuable screen space for items that will not be selected. For this reason, Visual Basic also includes the combo box control, which makes a nice alternative to the list box for certain types of selections.

The combo box has three unique formats that you can choose from when adding this control to the form:

- The drop-down combo box

- The simple combo box

- The drop-down list box

THE DROP-DOWN COMBO BOX

You create a drop-down combo box simply by adding a combo box to your form. The drop-down combo box style (0-Dropdown Combo) is this control's default format. When you look at Figure 6.2, you should notice right away some of the differences between the list box and the combo box. This combo box takes up less room and displays the list of items only when called upon (see Figure 6.3), closing back to its original size after a selection has been made. The default selection states -Select a City-. This was done by setting the Caption property of the combo box to that value. The value displayed after a selection is made is the selection itself, which removes the need for a separate text box or an additional list box to display the selected items.

FIGURE 6.2   A drop-down combo box.

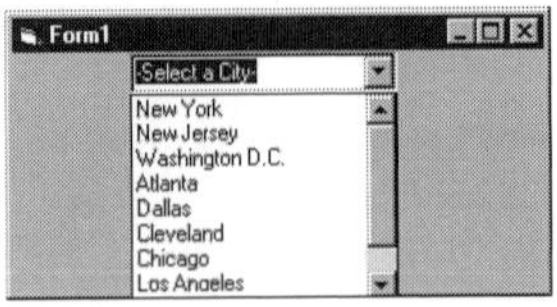

Figure 6.3   A drop-down combo box with the drop-down activated.

One of the benefits of this format is that the user can enter his or her own value into the selection area if the item they want is not in the list. This is true of all the combo box types you will review. This can sometimes lead to data problems that arise from typos (one person selects Dallas from the list, another types Dalas).

THE SIMPLE COMBO BOX

When adding a combo box to your form, you can change the Style property to 1 - Simple Combo, which will create a simple combo box. When you look at Figure 6.4, you might say to yourself, "Hey, that looks like a text box. Did I select the right control?".

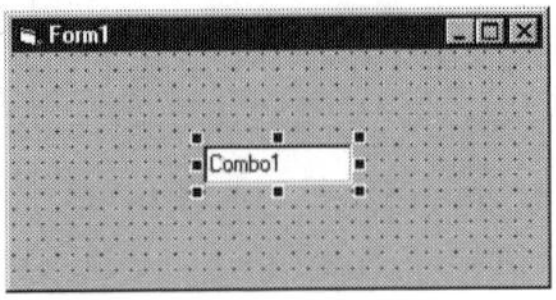

Figure 6.4   A simple combo box.

Before you delete it and try again, resize the combo box to see the entire control. Figure 6.5 shows what a simple combo box really looks like. As you can see, it resembles a list box with a text control at the top.

Just like the drop-down combo box, the default selection states -Select a City-. This was done by setting the Caption property of the combo box to that value. Drop-down combo boxes are more common because they take up less room on a form than do simple combo boxes; however, you might need to show a list all the time while allowing the user to enter new values.

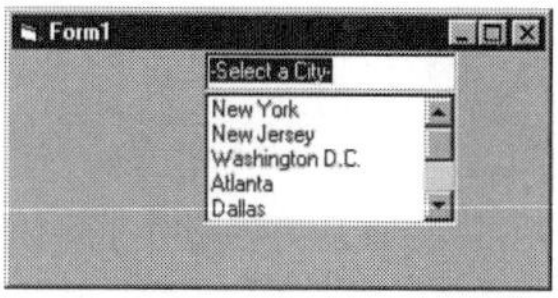

FIGURE 6.5   A simple combo box sized properly.

THE DROP-DOWN LIST COMBO BOX

The only difference between the drop-down list combo box and the drop-down combo box is that the user cannot add entries to the list or enter a value not on the list. You would create the drop-down list simple combo box by adding a combo box to your form, modifying the `Style` property of the control to `2 - Dropdown list Simple Combo`. Figures 6.6 and 6.7 represent examples of the drop-down list combo box before and after the drop-down.

FIGURE 6.6   A drop-down list combo box before the drop-down.

FIGURE 6.7   A drop-down list combo box after the drop-down.

THE TIMER CONTROL

One of the simplest and most misunderstood controls included with Visual Basic is the Timer control. This control can be used to provide any type of time-related processing within an application. If you use Microsoft Word or most other word processors, you have probably seen something called autosave. This is when the application will periodically save what you are working on.

You must do very little when using the Timer control. After you have placed it on the form (see Figure 6.8), it appears as a small icon that is invisible at runtime. There are only three properties that you should modify:

- The Name property

- The Interval property

- The Enabled property

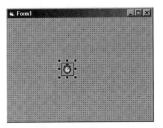

FIGURE 6.8   Adding the Timer control to a form.

As good programming practice, you should name the timer something that relates to its task, such as ClockTick if it will be used to update a clock display. To use the control, you need only set the Interval property to the number of milliseconds you want the timer to wait before executing the code in its Timer event routine. When the interval you set the Timer to expires, the Timer event is executed. The only way to turn off the timer is to set its Enabled property to False.

For example, if you want to have the color of the form blink every 15 seconds, you would add the following code:

```
Private Sub Form_Load()
    tmrBlink.Interval = 5000        '5 seconds in milliseconds
    tmrBlink.Enabled = True
End Sub
Private Sub tmrBlink_Timer()
    If Me.BackColor = &H8000000F Then
        Me.BackColor = vbRed
    Else
        Me.BackColor = &H8000000F
    End If
End Sub
```

As you can see, this control is very simple. However, you must think a little before actually using it because after it is started, it will continue to execute its code until it is disabled or the application ends.

SUMMARY

In this lesson you learned how to use list boxes, combo boxes, and timer controls to enhance your application. These controls enable you to create more sophisticated-looking applications with much neater and less cluttered forms.

LESSON 7
USING THE MsgBox AND InputBox FUNCTIONS

In this lesson, you learn how to use built-in message and input boxes. Message boxes let you display information to the user without changing the current form being displayed on the screen. Input boxes let you request input from the user without using another form.

THE MsgBox FUNCTION

Although you should be concerned with the way your output looks and how the user enters data, the message box is one of the best ways to display a message to the user during the execution of the application. Unlike controls on a form, the message box that appears will pop up as a dialog box. After the user reads the message displayed, he or she can click OK and continue with the process.

The message box not only displays data in a pop-up dialog, it can also display an icon or one or more action buttons for the user to choose from. It is capable of writing text data to the screen, which contains the message you want to display to the user. Figure 7.1 shows a sample dialog box generated with the MsgBox function. You can see that you control both the message and the title of the dialog box. You can also specify which icon is displayed and how many buttons will appear.

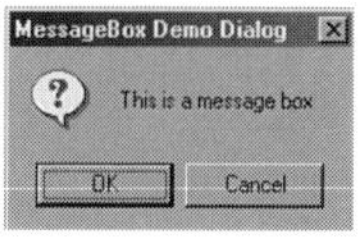

FIGURE 7.1   A message box is very similar to a small dialog box.

Note   A message box can be moved or closed but never resized.

USING THE MsgBox FUNCTION

The MsgBox function can be used in two different ways, as a function or as a statement. How the message box will be used dictates which of the two MsgBox options you will use. The following is the syntax of the two MsgBox options:

```
IntAnswer = MsgBox(strPrompt [, intStyle] [, strTitle])
```

and

```
MsgBox strPrompt [, intStyle] [, strTitle]
```

As you can see, the only real difference between the two is that the first one returns a value specifying which button was clicked, while the second one returns no value at all. The parameters of the function are described in the following paragraph.

strPrompt is a string expression (a constant string enclosed in quotation marks, a string variable, or a text control value) that you want displayed in the dialog box. If the string is long, the dialog box expands to hold the whole string, properly breaking each line between words. Figure 7.1's *strPrompt* would be "This is a message box."

Caution   The message box prompt text cannot be longer than 1,024 characters.

Other than the prompt value, all the remaining parameters are optional. The easiest kind of message box to display is one with only a message and an OK button. If you want to display such a message box, like the one shown in Figure 7.2, you don't have to specify the second and third values. This example is actually using the statement version of the MsgBox.

FIGURE 7.2   Simple message boxes require only the prompt.

When you specify only a prompt string, Visual Basic displays the prompt and uses the project name in the message box's title bar. The following code example would display the message box in Figure 7.2 when the application got to this line during the execution of the program:

```
MsgBox "This is a message box"
```

As you can see, a simple message box that only requires the user click OK is simple to produce. When a program must display such a message, a MsgBox statement is used to pop up the message box at that location in the code. The user will then see the message.

ADDING FUNCTIONALITY

The MsgBox's *intStyle* value is a numeric value or expression that controls the number of buttons as well as the icon that appear on the message box. The *strTitle* is the string that appears in the title bar.

The value you use for *intStyle* is made up of three values that describe

- The type and number of buttons displayed

- The icon displayed

- The default button

Tables 7.1, 7.2, and 7.3 contain the named constants that are used to set the `intStyle` value. Visual Basic makes these named constants available to you from anywhere in your application's code. Therefore, instead of coding a 3 for the message box's style value, you can use `vbYesNoCancel`. Internally, `vbYesNoCancel` is set to a value of 3, but `vbYesNoCancel` is easier for you to understand later if you must change the program because `vbYesNoCancel` is self-documenting and tells you that the value means that the three buttons—Yes, No, and Cancel—will appear in the message box.

TABLE 7.1   CHOOSING THE BUTTONS

NAME	VALUE	DESCRIPTION
vbOKOnly	0	Display OK button only
vbOKCancel	1	Display OK and Cancel buttons
vbAbortRetryIgnore	2	Display Abort, Retry, and Ignore buttons
vbYesNoCancel	3	Display Yes, No, and Cancel buttons
vbYesNo	4	Display Yes and No buttons
vbRetryCancel	5	Display Retry and Cancel buttons

TABLE 7.2   PICKING THE ICON

NAME	VALUE	DESCRIPTION
vbCritical	16	Display Critical Message icon
vbQuestion	32	Display Warning Query icon
vbExclamation	48	Display Warning Message icon
vbInformation	64	Display Information Message icon

Figure 7.3 shows the different icons that result from the values listed in Table 7.2.

FIGURE 7.3   The message box icons.

TABLE 7.3   SETTING THE DEFAULT BUTTON

NAME	VALUE	DESCRIPTION
vbDefaultButton1	0	First button is default.
vbDefaultButton2	256	Second button is default.
vbDefaultButton3	512	Third button is default.
VbDefaultButton4	768	Fourth button is default.

Table 7.1 describes the constants that you can use to specify the layout of the buttons on the dialog box. If no $intStyle$ value is specified, as in Figure 7.2, Visual Basic will use the default value of 0 for all three values. If you want a style of buttons different from the default OK button, use a different value from Table 7.1.

If you want an icon to appear in the dialog box, add one of the values from Table 7.2 to the $intStyle$ value from Table 7.1. So, to get the OK and Cancel buttons and the Warning Query icon to display, you could specify the value 33 for the $intStyle$ parameter. The value of 33 is the sum of the 1-OKCancel and the 32-vbQuestion as shown in the following code.

```
MsgBox "This is a message box",33
```

However, the constants can be used instead of the numeric values. So the 33 can be replaced with the following statement:

```
MsgBox "This is a message box", vbOKCancel + vbQuestion
```

A dialog box will always contain a default button that appears outlined to look as if it is selected. In other words, the button has the focus. If the user presses Enter without selecting another button first, the default button will be clicked. Therefore, if you want the Cancel button to be the default button when the dialog box appears, add the constant vbDefaultButton2 to the *intStyle* value.

> **Note** Message boxes use the Windows Sound set-
> tings. So, if the user has set a specific sound for one of
> the message box icons, such as the Critical Warning
> icon, that sound will be heard when the message box
> is displayed.

INTERACTING WITH THE MsgBox

Although the MsgBox is useful for displaying messages, there will be times when your application will need to know which button the user clicked when the dialog box was closed. If only the OK button was displayed, your program knows that the user clicked the OK button. However, if the message box contains additional buttons, your program must be able to respond to the button that the user clicked.

> **Note** The execution of your application stops when-
> ever a message box is displayed. The MsgBox function
> triggers the display of the message box, and no other
> code in the application can execute until the user
> closes the message box by clicking one of the dis-
> played buttons.

The returned value will indicate which button the user clicked. So, when the MsgBox function displays several buttons, your program can determine which button was clicked by testing the return value. The values that can be returned by the MsgBox function are listed in Table 7.4.

TABLE 7.4   THE RETURN VALUES OF THE MsgBox FUNCTION

NAME	VALUE	DESCRIPTION
vbOK	1	The user clicked OK
vbCancel	2	The user clicked Cancel
vbAbort	3	The user clicked Abort
vbRetry	4	The user clicked Retry
vbIgnore	5	The user clicked Ignore
vbYes	6	The user clicked Yes
vbNo	7	The user clicked No

When Visual Basic executes the following statement, the program waits
for the user to respond to the MsgBox by clicking one of the displayed buttons. The resulting choice, a numeric value from Table 7.4, is then
assigned to the variable *intAnswer*.

```
intAnswer = MsgBox("Are you ready?", vbYesNoCancel +
➥vbQuestion)
```

The vbYesNoCancel code sends the Yes, No, and Cancel buttons to the
message box and vbQuestion displays the Warning Query icon. If the user
chooses Yes, the *intAnswer* variable is assigned the value 6 (vbYes).
intAnswer gets a 7 (vbNo) if the user chooses No, and *intAnswer* gets a 2
(vbCancel) if the user chooses Cancel. Although your program will work
using the actual numbers, you will want to use the constants instead.

Don't confuse the return value with the button value used in the function
itself. For example, the return value might be 3 (vbAbort) and you might
have used 3 (vbYesNoCancel) to describe the buttons that you want displayed. So, after the message box is displayed, the return value might
overlap one of your message box values. However, the numbers' mean-
ings are totally different. After the program gains control from the message box function, it will test the returned value to determine what action
the user requested.

If the Esc key is pressed on any message box that contains a Cancel button, Visual Basic returns the value 2 (vbCancel) from the MsgBox function.

By using the IF...EndIf statement or the Select Case statement
(described in Lesson 12), the program can check which button was
clicked and take the appropriate action.

THE InputBox FUNCTION

The InputBox gets data from the user by displaying a dialog box with a
text box on it. Of course, the MsgBox also gets data from the user, but it is
only the return value of the button that was clicked. The InputBox is the
opposite of the MsgBox function. Whereas the MsgBox has a primary purpose of displaying data to the user, the InputBox is designed to get data
from the user.

When your program must interact with the user, you can use an input box.
Figure 7.4 shows an example of an input box. As you can see, an input
box contains a title bar, a prompt, command buttons, and a text box area
to receive user input.

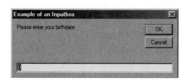

FIGURE 7.4   An example of an InputBox.

You are well aware of the ease with which forms enable users to enter
data; however, you also must have a way to ask the user questions without
using another form.

USING THE InputBox FUNCTION

The following code shows the syntax of an input box. It is very similar to
the message box. However, there are a few unique differences.

```
strAnswer = InputBox(strPrompt [, strTitle] [, strDefault]
➡[, intXpos] [, intYpos])
```

If you leave out either the strTitle or the strDefault (or both), the com-
mas are still required as placeholders. The strPrompt is a text value that
you want displayed so that the user knows what is required.

> **Tip**   Always ask the user a question or describe the input you want. If you don't, the user will have no way of knowing what to enter in response to the input box.

The *strPrompt* cannot be longer than 1,024 characters. The *strTitle* is used for the input box's title, and Visual Basic displays the application's name for the title if you don't specify one. The *strDefault* is the default string that would appear in the text box. This allows the user to either accept that value or change it. The user would accept the default value by pressing Enter.

intXpos and *intYpos* allow you to position the InputBox dialog in a specific location on the screen, where *intXPos* is the x coordinate or horizontal position, and *intYPos* is the y coordinate or the vertical position on the screen.

When the user enters a response in the input box and clicks the **OK** button, the variable indicated at *strAnswer* will hold the user's answer. If the user presses Esc or clicks the **Cancel** button, a null or empty value would be returned.

Figure 7.5 shows an input box that was generated from the following InputBox function:

```
strUserName = InputBox("What is your name?", "Getting a
➥name", "Enter Name Here")
If strUserName <> "" Then
    MsgBox "Hello " & strUserName
Else
    Msgbox "The Input function was Cancelled"
End If
```

The preceding example also shows how to check to see whether the Cancel button was clicked and respond accordingly.

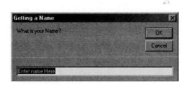

FIGURE 7.5   An example of an InputBox.

SUMMARY

This lesson covered two very important functions, MsgBox and InputBox, which are used in almost every Windows application there is. The MsgBox can be seen whenever a message must be displayed or a decision must be made by the user. In addition, when the application requires a single input value of some sort, the InputBox is often used in place of more complicated, user-designed forms to obtain the required information from the user.

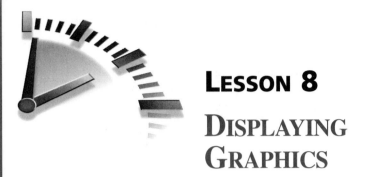

LESSON 8

DISPLAYING GRAPHICS

In this lesson, you will see how to use the Picture Box, Image, and Animation controls.

In order to "jazz up" an application, many programmers add pictures, graphics, or animation. The addition of these images makes the application easier to learn and sometimes more pleasant to look at.

The simplest thing to do with graphics in your application is to add a picture as the background for a form (see Figure 8.1). You do this by setting the Picture property of the form object to the name of a picture file to be used instead of a color, which would normally be set using the BackColor property. The thing to be careful of here is that unlike Windows wallpaper, which can be tiled (copied over and over again to complete the pattern) or stretched to fit, your image will be displayed only once on the form. You must be sure that your image is large enough to cover the portion of the form you want to be covered.

FIGURE 8.1 A form with a picture as a background.

Two controls exist to let you add graphics to your form: the Image control and the Picture Box control. The difference between the two is that the Image control is more efficient in the way it uses the available resources of the computer (it runs better on a slower machine), whereas the Picture Box control offers more programmatic control (there are more things you can do to it). Table 8.1 lists the image types supported by both.

TABLE 8.1 IMAGE TYPES SUPPORTED BY PICTURE BOX AND IMAGE CONTROLS

TYPE	EXTENSION
Bitmap	.BMP
Cursor	.CUR
Graphics Interchange Format	.GIF
Icons	.ICO
JPEG files	.JPG or .JPEG
Metafiles	.WMF

THE PICTURE BOX CONTROL

You add the Picture Box control to your form by double-clicking it in your toolbox (see Figure 8.2). You then modify the Picture property of the control to represent the image you want to display on the form. This is done either programmatically (using the LoadPicture statement) or by clicking the ellipsis (...) and browsing to find the image to use.

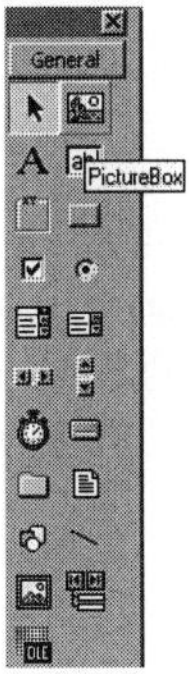

FIGURE 8.2   The Picture Box control.

> **Tip** Visual Basic 6 includes a large number of graphics files for your use. These are found in the c:\Program Files\Microsoft Visual Studio\ Common\ Graphics directory structure.

Figure 8.3 shows a picture box added to a form. As you can see from the example, you can add an image to your form and change the size of the picture box. However, the picture box is only a placeholder, and changing its size does not stretch the image. Visual Basic provides an Autosize property but this goes the other way and resizes the object to the size of the image.

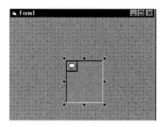

FIGURE 8.3 A picture box.

> **Note** When you use LoadPicture to load an image at runtime, the LoadPicture statement takes the form of
>
> ```
> LoadPicture([GraphicFileName] [,varSize]
> ➥[,varColorDepth] [,varX,varY])
> ```
>
> or as an example:
>
> ```
> imgClipboard.Picture=LoadPicture("c:\program files\
> ➥microsoft visual studio\common\graphics\
> ➥metafiles\business\clipbord.wmf")
> ```

THE IMAGE CONTROL

You add the Image control to your form by double-clicking it in your toolbox (see Figure 8.4). You then modify the `Picture` property of the control to represent the image you want to display on the form. You can do this either programmatically (by using `LoadPicture`) or by clicking the ellipsis (...) and browsing to find the image to use. Figure 8.5 shows a picture added to the form using the Image control. As you can see from the example, because you used an Image control you can add an image to the form, change the size of the Image control, and force the image to stretch to the Image control's size.

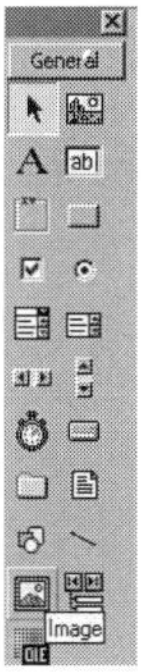

FIGURE 8.4   The Image control.

FIGURE 8.5   An Image control.

Caution If you want to stretch an image to a new size or dimension, be sure to first set the Image control's Stretch property to True and then change the Width and Height properties as desired.

USING THE ANIMATION CONTROL

If you've been using Windows for any length of time, you're probably familiar with the animations used to inform you of some action being done, such as the delete process shown in Figure 8.6. The Animation control enables you to provide the same functionality within your application. It enables you to display silent .AVI clips, miniature movies shown sequentially to create the animation. These animations run as background tasks, which allows your application to keep processing whatever is required.

FIGURE 8.6   A delete process shown with an animation.

The Animation control is one of two controls contained in the Windows Common Controls 2 file (MSCOMCT2.OCX). To use the Animation control, you first must add it to your toolbox through the Components dialog box. After it is in the toolbox, you can add the control to the form that needs the animation displayed. Figure 8.7 shows the Animation control in the toolbox.

Putting the Animation control on the form gives your application a container in which the animation sequence can play. To run the animation, however, you must create some code to open the .AVI file and start the playback process. The control's Open method is used to open the file specified as the argument for the method. The .AVI files included with VB6 are installed in the \PROGRAM FILES\MICROSOFT VISUAL STUDIO\COMMON\GRAPHICS\VIDEOS directory. After you open the file, you must execute the `Play` method to start the animation. The follow-ing code shows how to open and then play an animation file:

```
strAVIFile = "C:\Program Files\MICROSOFT VISUAL STUDIO\COMMON\
➥GRAPHICS\VIDEOS\Filecopy.avi"
anmAnimation1.Open strAVIFile
anmAnimation1.Play
```

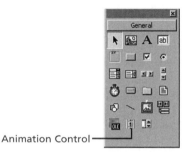

Animation Control

FIGURE 8.7   The Animation control in the toolbox.

When you're ready to stop the animation, you simply execute the control's `Stop` method:

```
anmAnimation1.Stop
```

To try out this control, start a new project and add the control and two command buttons to the default form (see Figure 8.8). Next, change the names of the command buttons to `cmdStart` and `cmdStop`, respectively. Now add the preceding code segments to the appropriate button click rou-tines (see Figure 8.9).

Finally, execute your application and click the **Start** button. You should see the file copy animation as shown in Figure 8.10. When you're ready, click the **Stop** button to end the animation.

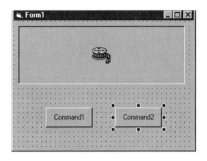

FIGURE 8.8   Working with Animations.

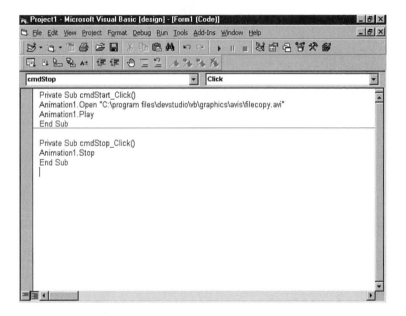

FIGURE 8.9   Adding the code for the Animation control.

In addition to playing the animation until the Stop method is executed, you can set three optional parameters of the Animation control:

- Repeat—Specifies the number of times the animation will be repeated.

- Start—Sets the frame where the animation will start.
- Stop—Sets the frame where the animation will end.

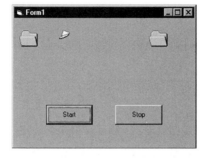

FIGURE 8.10   Giving the user status about the file copy process.

You can specify any or all the optional parameters. If any are omitted, however, the default values are used. If you omit one of the parameters, you must use a comma as a placeholder. To modify the code in the preceding example to play the animation four times and only the first 10 frames, you should change the Play method as shown:

anmAnimation1.Open strAVIFile, 4,,10

Finally, it's a good practice to use the Close method when you're finished using an animation file. However, it's not necessary to close one file before opening another.

SUMMARY

In this lesson, you learned how to use the Picture Box and Image controls to display different types of pictures in your application. In addition, you learned how to use the Animation control, which enables you to display moving images and give the user feedback when needed.

LESSON 9

PROGRAMMING WITH EVENTS

This lesson shows you how to create complex applications with a small amount of effort by using Visual Basic events.

As you have seen in previous lessons, everything that happens within Windows is accomplished using something called an event. Because events are an integral part of the Windows operating system, you must first understand what an event is and what event-driven programming design really means. This chapter shows you how Visual Basic events help you create complex applications with a small amount of effort.

UNDERSTANDING WINDOWS EVENTS

Events are in everything: a ringing phone, a sporting event, and a ringing alarm clock. These events and many more are handled according to their importance. When the phone rings, you probably answer it. When the alarm goes off, you wake up unless it is the weekend. So you see, you are surrounded by hundreds of events at all times. The difference is that you respond only to the ones you feel are important at the moment.

Taking this back to Visual Basic and Windows, when a user is executing an application in Windows, she triggers many different events. She presses keys, moves the mouse, clicks an object, and so on. The program is expected to understand which event just occurred and then take some action. Given the many events that can occur in Windows, this is not an easy task.

Before the Windows environment was developed, most computer programs were started, ran through a sequential process, and ended by producing a report of some type. When online or interactive programs became popular, the process did not change very much. The user was presented with a short list of options to select from, and then whichever option was selected was processed in the same sequential process.

Now, with Windows, an application will "wait" for something to happen. Actually, Windows receives every action, known as a message, that occurs on the computer and then passes it on to the program for which it is meant. So, if the user clicks the mouse in the application window, Windows notices it. Windows then sends that application a message indicating that the event occurred, along with some additional information, such as the parameters of the event.

THE EVENT PROCEDURE

Knowing when an event occurs is the first step in using them in your application. When the user types something on the keyboard or uses the mouse, Windows will receive the input from the event and then pass it on to the application. Your application then must decide how to react to that event. As discussed in the preceding section, you must respond only to the events that are important to your application. You ignore an event simply by not adding any code to its event procedure. Every object that you have in your application has one or more events associated with it. Figure 9.1 shows the Code Editor with the drop-down events list for the form.

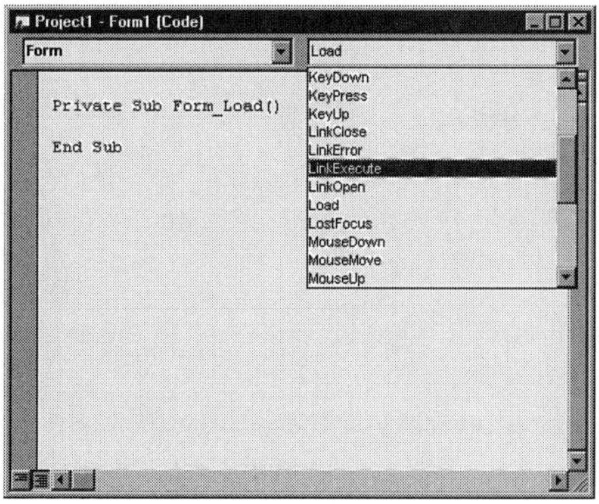

FIGURE 9.1   Choosing the events to respond to.

If you created a new project and executed it without adding any code, nothing would happen when you clicked the mouse on the form. However, if you added even a single line of code to the form's Click event procedure, it would be executed when the mouse was clicked.

TRIGGERING EVENTS

In a Windows application, two different types of events can occur. The first type is a user event; that is, something that the user does that triggers the event. The second type is a system event, or something that occurs within the application or Windows that is not controlled by the user. These system events include

- Timer actions

- Data access errors

- Form status changes

- Control status changes

As you can see, triggering an event controls all the actions in your program. Because of this, there are usually many ways for the user to trigger the same event. For example, the `Click` event can be triggered in response to several other events besides just left-clicking the mouse on an object. The following are some of the other ways to trigger a `Click` event:

- Clicking the right mouse button on certain controls.

- Pressing the space bar if a command button has the focus.

- Pressing the Enter key if the command button's `Default` property is `True`.

- Pressing the Esc key if the command button's `Cancel` property is `True`.

- Pressing a hotkey if it has been defined in the `Caption` property.

From the preceding short list, you can see that there are a variety of ways to trigger a `Click` event. This gives you the control needed to complete a Visual Basic application.

MOUSE AND KEYBOARD EVENTS

Many events can be triggered using the mouse. Each of them enables you to respond to them as needed. The mouse-oriented events are listed as follows:

- Click—Occurs when a user presses the left mouse button.

- DblClick—Occurs when the user presses the left mouse button twice in rapid succession, without moving the mouse.

- DragDrop—Occurs when the mouse button is held down and dragged to another control that has DragDrop enabled. Visual Basic responds by executing the DragDrop procedure for the target object.

- DragOver—Occurs when the user is in the process of dragging an object.

- MouseDown—Occurs when a mouse button is pressed.

- MouseUp—Occurs when a mouse button is released.

- MouseMove—Occurs when the mouse is moved over an object with no buttons pressed.

To see an example of these triggers, start a new project and place a text box and command button on the form as shown in Figure 9.2.

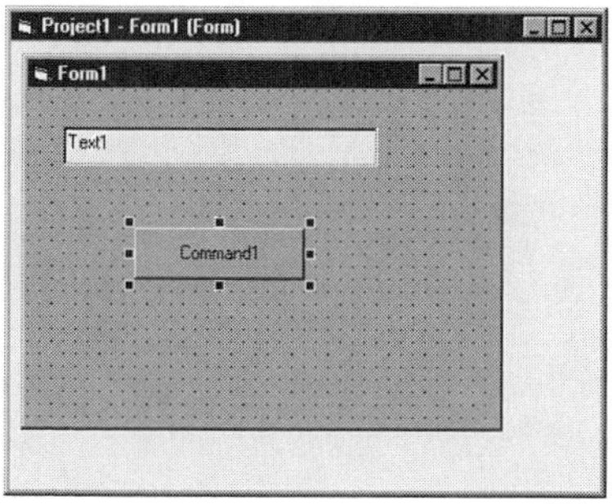

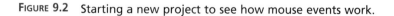

FIGURE 9.2   Starting a new project to see how mouse events work.

Again, without code, this program will do nothing. Add the code in Listing 9.1 to display a message in the text box when the mouse is moved over it and clear that message if the mouse is anywhere else.

LISTING 9.1   MOUSEMOVE.TXT—USING THE MOUSEMOVE EVENT TO
INTERACT WITH THE USER

```
Private Sub Form_MouseMove(Button As Integer, Shift As
➥Integer, X As Single, Y As Single)
    Text1.Text = ""
End Sub

Private Sub Command1_MouseMove(Button As Integer,
➥Shift As Integer, X As Single, Y As Single)
    Text1.Text = "This is a Text Box"
End Sub
```

Now, run the application and move the mouse over the command button.
You will see a message displayed in the text box. Then, move the mouse
away from the command button and the text box will be cleared.

Using the available mouse events with other events in the application will
provide you with the control needed to produce the professional look and
feel to your program that users have come to expect from a Windows
application.

KEYBOARD EVENTS

Keyboard events enable the program to monitor any keyboard input that is
passed to a program, and to validate and modify that input if needed. The
main purpose of these events is input validation. The following three main
events are associated with the keyboard:

- KeyPress—Occurs when a key is pressed but before the program
  actually processes it.
- KeyDown—Occurs when a key is pressed.
- KeyUp—Occurs when a key is released.

These events give you the control needed to verify input in a professional
manner. If a user presses a letter key when a numeric key is expected, the
program should display an error message and then allow the user to correct the error, as shown in the next section.

OTHER EVENTS

Many other events that you can use in your application are useful to perform certain actions when something starts or changes. Visual Basic was written to trap several state-change events so that your program will have a chance to respond if needed. The following are some of the events in this group:

- Activate—Occurs when a form becomes the active window
- Deactivate—Occurs when a form is no longer the active window
- GotFocus—Occurs when an object becomes the one in focus
- LostFocus—Occurs when the focus is moved to another control
- Load—Occurs the first time a form is loaded
- Unload—Occurs when the form is unloaded

By using these and many more status events, you can manage your applications with a great deal of control and enhanced appearance.

VALIDATING TEXT BOX INPUT

After you understand what events are, you can start combining them to create the complex actions required for your application. To see how all the different events work together, this section builds a fairly simple text input routine using several of the events previously discussed in this chapter.

You will create the complete process from the moment the user clicks on the text box to when the user clicks somewhere else. To see this, use the project that you previously created and set its properties as listed in Table 9.1.

TABLE 9.1   PROPERTY SETTINGS FOR THE PROJECT

OBJECT	PROPERTY	VALUE
Form	Caption	Validating Text Input
	Name	frmEvent

continues

TABLE 9.1   CONTINUED

OBJECT	PROPERTY	VALUE
Text box	Name	txtInput
	Text	<Blank>
Command button	Caption	Quit
	Name	cmdQuit

SETTING UP THE INPUT

In most applications, when you click on a text box or move to it, any text displayed is highlighted. This is done using the GotFocus event. This event is triggered whenever the associated object gets control, usually by having the user click in the input area. The code in Listing 9.2 uses the SelLength and SelStart properties to highlight any text already present.

LISTING 9.2   GOTFOCUS.TXT—RESPONDING TO THE GotFocus EVENT

```
Private Sub txtInput_GotFocus()
    txtInput.SelStart = 0
    txtInput.SelLength = Len(txtInput.Text)
End Sub
```

Now, whenever the focus or control is passed to the text box, its contents are highlighted as shown in Figure 9.3.

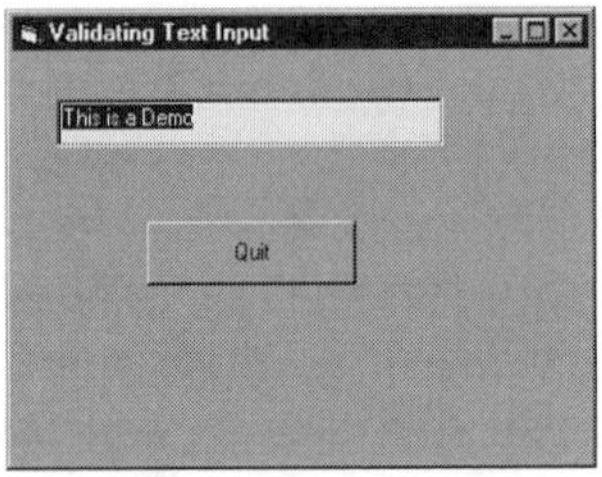

FIGURE 9.3   Highlighted text when the text box receives the focus.

VERIFYING INPUT

After the text box has the focus, the next step is to process whatever text was entered. There are two methods that you could use to perform this task. The first and simpler of the two is to simply check the finished input when the user is finished and the focus leaves the text box. The second method has you checking the input character by character to prevent invalid data from being entered.

They might sound the same to you, but consider a date input. The user could enter valid characters, such as 9/40/99. Unfortunately, this is not a valid date. Or, the user could enter invalid characters, such as Oct/22/98. This is not only an invalid date, but would cause an error if the ISDATE function was used to validate the input.

The first step in validating the input is to ensure that only valid characters are entered. This can be done using the KeyPress event. This event is used to preview each keystroke before it is accepted by the program. If the character is not valid, it is ignored. Listing 9.3 shows the KeyPress event code for a numeric value that contains four digits and only one decimal point. The KeyPress routine passes the numeric value of the pressed key in the KeyAscii parameter. This parameter is then used to check for valid characters. In addition, the routine uses the InStr function to search the entered string for any occurrences of the period character.

LISTING 9.3 **KEYPRESS.TXT—CHECKING THE CHARACTERS ENTERED FROM THE KEYBOARD**

```
Private Sub txtInput_KeyPress(KeyAscii As Integer)
If (KeyAscii < 48 Or KeyAscii > 58) And KeyAscii <> 8
➥And KeyAscii <> 46 Then
    Beep
    KeyAscii = 0
End If
If Len(txtInput.Text) > 4 Then
    Beep
    KeyAscii = 0
End If
If KeyAscii = 46 Then
    If InStr(1, txtInput.Text, ".") > 0 Then
        Beep
        KeyAscii = 0
    End If
End If
End Sub
```

VALIDATING KEY INPUT

As already described in the preceding section, the final step is to validate the value in the text box after the user is finished entering information. This is usually performed when control is passed to another object or a command button is clicked. Your program will recognize when this happens by using the text box's LostFocus event. By placing a validation code in this event, you can either accept the value or display an error to the user and start the input process again. The code in Listing 9.4 shows the validation of the input value to make sure it is between 0 and 25 by using the CSng function to convert the text value into a single precision number. If it is not, a message is displayed and the focus returns to the text box.

LISTING 9.4   **LOSTFOCUS.TXT—VALIDATING THE FINAL INPUT VALUE**

```
Private Sub txtInput_LostFocus()
If CSng(txtInput.Text) < 0 Or CSng(txtInput.Text) > 26 Then
    MsgBox "The number entered is Invalid", vbCritical,
    ➥"Input Validate Demo"
    txtInput.SetFocus
End If
End Sub
```

TESTING THE PROCESS

After you have added the code to the form, try executing the program and entering valid and invalid characters to see how the code you have added responds to the events.

> **Plain English** Although this example shows you how to combine different events to form a process, you should always look to see whether Visual Basic provides an easier method. In the case of text box input, the keyboard preview and form validation that was performed in the KeyPress event procedure can be replaced using the MaskedEdit control.

SUMMARY

By using the event-driven programming concept, you can develop systems that respond to the way people do their work. It enables you to concentrate on one control and the events that can affect it. By adding code to the events, you can write programs that monitor and react to any event that might occur while your program is being used. You have seen how your program responds to events passed to it from Windows. Finally, you learned how to combine the different events to create a complex process for the application.

LESSON 10
ASSIGNING PROPERTIES

In this lesson, you learn how to change the look and actions of your application by changing the properties, methods, and events of the objects in the application.

PROPERTIES—AN OVERVIEW

All objects in Visual Basic are controlled by their properties, methods, and events. Although this lesson focuses on setting the properties of an object, the basic principles used to access the properties also apply to an object's methods and events. For more information on setting the methods and events of an object, read Lesson 9, "Programming with Events."

Each unique object in Visual Basic has its own set of properties that let you control how the object interacts with the other objects in the application. The majority of the objects in Visual Basic have the following properties in common:

- `Left`
- `Top`
- `Height`
- `Width`
- `Name`
- `Enabled`
- `Visible`

> **Plain English**   When reading this lesson, references are made to both objects and controls. The term *objects*, in this lesson, refers to the entire collection of controls, forms, classes, and so on. The term *controls*, in this lesson, refers to the specific control class.

Every control has one particular property that is used more than the others (for example, the Text property for a text box or the Caption property for a label). Visual Basic has defined that particular property (depending on the control) as the default property for that control. This property is then referenced when using a control without specifying an exact property. Table 10.1 lists the common controls and their default properties. The example shown in Listing 10.1 illustrates how the default property would be used.

LISTING 10.1   **LOGIN.FRM—THE TEXT CONTROL HAS THE DEFAULT PROPERTY OF Text**

```
Private Sub Form_Load()
    txtUserName = "Please Log in."

End Sub
```

The code in Listing 10.1 will display the phrase Please Log In in the txtUserName text box of the logon form.

TABLE 10.1   **DEFAULT PROPERTIES OF COMMON CONTROLS**

CONTROL	VALUE
Check box	Value
Combo box	Text
Directory list box	Path
Drive list box	Drive
File list box	FileName
Horizontal scrollbar	Value

CONTROL	VALUE
Image	Picture
Label	Caption
Option button	Value
Picture box	Picture
Text box	Text
Vertical scrollbar	Value

In the next few sections, you will take a look at how to change properties using the Property dialog box and code.

SPECIFYING PROPERTIES OF THE LOGON FORM

To follow along with the topics in this section, you will be using the logon form template that is included with Visual Basic. Start a new project and add the logon form to it. Then, double-click the form to display it in the Forms window. Although you will be using the Logon form, the principles apply to whatever form or control supports the discussed properties.

REFERENCING FORMS AND CONTROLS FROM CODE

When you are creating a project in Visual Basic, the first form object you create is given the name of Form1. The first command button that you create is given the name of command1, and so on for any other controls that you create. As you create the second and third instances of these objects, you will probably notice that Visual Basic names these subsequent objects consecutively, as command1, command2, command3, and so on. As your application grows, it can be difficult to remember what each command button controls.

To help you solve this problem, each object—whether it is a form or control—uses the Name property to distinguish itself from the other objects in your application.

As you start naming the different objects on a form, it is good programming style to name them using a standard set of naming conventions so the type of object they represent can easily be identified in code. Table 3.1 in Lesson 3, "Creating Your First Application Project," provides a suggested list of prefixes for some of the common controls in Visual Basic. For any controls that are not listed, you should use a unique prefix that is easy to recognize in code.

CHANGING THE FORM SIZE

You can control the size of the form either by manually changing the Height and Width properties at design and runtime or by selecting the form and dragging the sizing handles at design time. The Height property represents the form's vertical size on the screen, whereas the Width property represents the form's horizontal size on the screen, as shown in Figure 10.1.

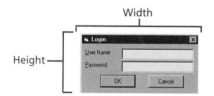

FIGURE 10.1   The Height and Width properties control the overall size of the object.

To change the Height and Width properties at design time, you can change the Height property in the Properties window simply by selecting the existing value and typing a new one, as shown in Figure 10.2. You can change the Width property in a similar manner.

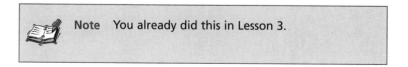

Note   You already did this in Lesson 3.

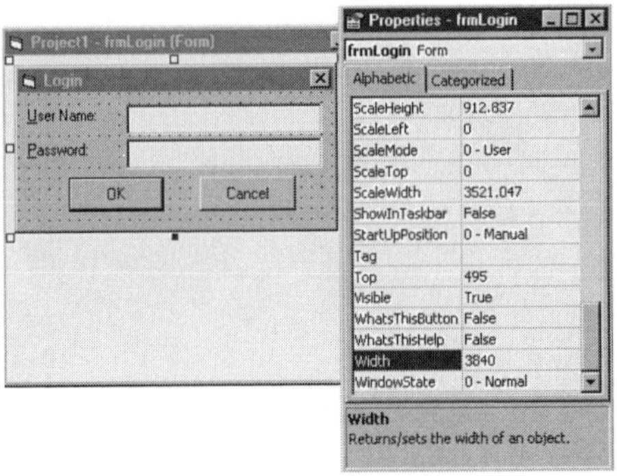

FIGURE 10.2   The Properties dialog box enables you to change the available properties at design time.

To change the Height and Width properties at runtime, place the code in Listing 10.2 in the Form_Activate event of the login form. The Form_Activate event is executed whenever the login form is initialized or gets focus.

LISTING 10.2   LOGIN.FRM—THE Height AND Width CAN BE CHANGED AT RUNTIME VIA CODE

```
Private Sub Form_Activate()

    frmLogin.Height = 2500
    frmLogin.Width = 5000

End Sub
```

When you press F5 to run your application, you will notice that the login form has changed its height and width.

Notice in Listing 10.2 that the login form is referred to by name. Although there is nothing wrong with this style of coding, take a look at Listing 10.3.

LISTING 10.3   LOGIN.FRM—Me REFERENCE

```
Private Sub Form_Activate()

    Me.Height = 2500
    Me.Width = 5000

End Sub
```

Notice that the code is unchanged except that you have replaced the name of the form with the keyword ME. ME is used by Visual Basic to refer to the currently loaded form object. The code in Listing 10.3 is not tied to a specific form, and as a result can be reused in other form objects that have the same Height and Width property requirements.

SETTING THE POSITION

In addition to controlling the form's height and width, you also have control over its position on the screen during runtime. You can control the relative position of the form during design time by manually changing the Top and Left properties in the Properties dialog box or by selecting the form and dragging the sizing handles at design time. The Top property represents the distance from the top edge of the object to the top of its container. The Left property represents the distance from the left side of the object to the left side of the object container. This is shown in Figure 10.3.

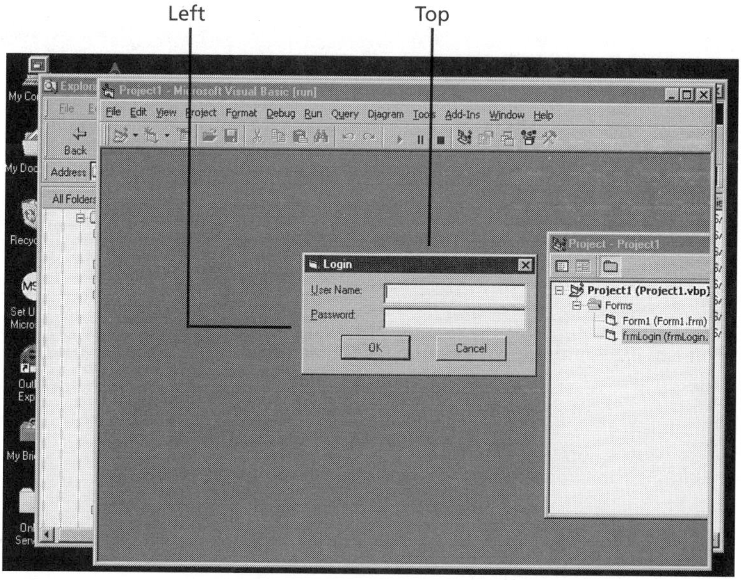

FIGURE 10.3 The Top and Left properties control the form placement on the screen.

Again, you can make changes at design time by using the Properties dialog box. To change the Top and Left properties at design time, simply select the desired property value and type in the new value. When you run your application, the new property values will be used.

> **Note** The Top and Left properties relate directly to the available client area of the screen. In an MDI application, the client window is determined by the size of the MDI form. In a non-MDI application, the client area refers to the available screen display area.

To make changes at runtime, you will need to add some code segments to your application. Typically, these code segments are not more than a few lines in length, but they give you total programmatic control over how the form or control is positioned during runtime. The code in Listing 10.4 adjusts the Top and Left properties so that the form is positioned in the upper-left corner of your screen.

LISTING 10.4   LOGIN.FRM—THE Top AND Left PROPERTIES ALLOW YOU TO POSITION THE FORM RELATIVE TO ITS CONTAINER

```
Private Sub Form_Load()

    frmLogin.Top = 0
    frmLogin.Left = 0

End Sub
```

You can use similar code to control the placement of controls on a form. Any control that has a Top or Left property can be moved on the form at runtime. The code in Listing 10.5 provides an example of moving the login form's command buttons.

LISTING 10.5   LOGIN.FRM—OBJECTS THAT SUPPORT THE Top AND Left PROPERTIES CAN BE MOVED IN A SIMILAR FASHION

```
Private Sub Form_Load()

  cmdOK.Top = 567.2
```

```
cmdOK.Left = 112.674

cmdCancel.Top = 567.2
cmdCancel.Left = 2366.144
```

```
End Sub
```

CONTROLLING USER RESPONSE

There might be cases in which you want to limit the choices available to a user of your application. For example, suppose you want the Login form to display the Cancel button only after the user has entered a letter into the txtUserName text box.

The Visible and Enabled properties enable you to control which objects are accessible during specific application activities. Using the Login form as an example, assume that you want the Cancel button to be available only after the user has entered a login ID. To see how this property works, add the code in Listing 10.6 and run the project.

LISTING 10.6   LOGIN.FRM—THE Visible PROPERTY CAN BE USED WITH THE Top AND Left PROPERTIES TO REDESIGN AN INTERFACE DURING RUNTIME

```
Private Sub Form_Load()
    cmdCancel.Visible = False

End Sub


Private Sub txtUserName_Change()
    cmdCancel.Visible = True

End Sub
```

The code in Listing 10.6 will display the Login form as shown in Figure 10.4. Notice that the Cancel button's Visible property is set to False when the form is loaded and is then set to True when the txtUserName control changes. In normal use, you probably would want the Cancel button to remain visible but have any actions connected to the button active only after a certain event has occurred. This way, the user understands that additional options are available but they are currently not active. This process can be accomplished with the Enabled property. The Enabled property will allow the object to be displayed; however, any text on the object will be grayed out, indicating that the object—in this case the **Cancel** button—has been disabled. To see how this property works, add the code in Listing 10.7 and run the project.

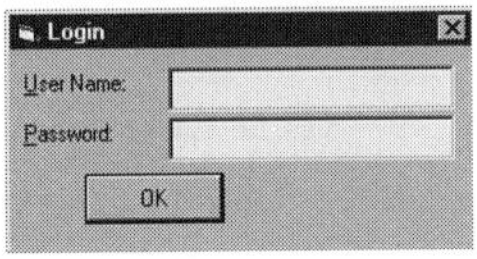

FIGURE 10.4   The Login form with the **Cancel** button invisible.

LISTING 10.7   **LOGIN.FRM**—THIS SAME TYPE OF CODE SEGMENT CAN BE USED WITH OTHER OBJECTS THAT SUPPORT THE **Enabled** PROPERTY

```
Private Sub Form_Load()
    cmdCancel.Enabled = False

End Sub

Private Sub txtUserName_Change()
    cmdCancel.Enabled = True

End Sub
```

This code will display the Login form as shown in Figure 10.5. Notice that the **Cancel** button's Enabled property has been set to False when the form loads and is then set to True when the user types a value into the txtUserName control. This way, the user is aware of the **Cancel** button but cannot click it until a login ID is entered. The previous examples concentrated on command buttons and how to control their properties through code. However, this same concept can be used with forms and other controls that support dynamic property assignments in your application.

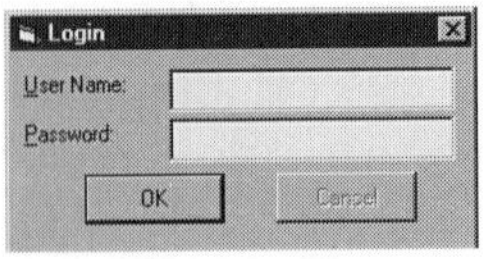

FIGURE 10.5   The Login form with the text of the **Cancel** button grayed out, indicating a control that cannot be selected.

SPECIFYING PROPERTIES OF A CONTROL

Setting a control's properties with the Properties dialog box can satisfy a lot of your application's needs. However, you must also be able to set the properties at runtime. In addition, you must be able to get the property values for a control. The previous examples focused on changing the properties of an object. In the following example, you will discover how you can modify the flow of the program based on the property settings of an object in your application.

There will be occasions where you will need a particular object on a form to perform different actions based on a user- or program-initiated event. For example, suppose you want the Login form to display a **Reset** button after a user began typing in the `txtUserName` control; however, if the user entered the name of SuperUser, a **Cancel** button would be displayed. You could add another button to the form and use the `Visible` property to display the correct button, or you can use the existing controls on the Login form. The code in Listing 10.8 shows how to modify the `Caption` property to perform this task.

LISTING 10.8   LOGIN.FRM—PROPERTIES CAN BE CHANGED AT RUNTIME BASED ON A SPECIFIC USER- OR PROGRAM-GENERATED EVENT

```
Private Sub Form_Load()
    cmdCancel.Enabled = False

End Sub

Private Sub txtUserName_Change()
    cmdCancel.Caption = "Reset"

    If txtUserName = "SuperUser" Then
        cmdCancel.Enabled = True
        cmdCancel.Caption = "Cancel"
    Else
        cmdCancel.Enabled = True
    End If
End Sub

Private Sub cmdCancel_Click()

    Select Case cmdCancel.Caption
```

```
Case Is = "Cancel"
    cmdCancel.Enabled = True
    Me.Hide
Case Is = "Reset"
    txtUserName = ""
    txtPassword = ""
    txtUserName.SetFocus

End Select

End Sub
```

> **Note**   The code in the `cmdCancel_Click` event is an altered version of the default code supplied with the default Login dialog box that comes with Visual Basic 6.

One function of this code is to disable the `cmdCancel` button when the Login form is initially loaded. The form will then be displayed with the caption of the `cmdCancel` button changed to Reset, as shown in Figure 10.6 when a user enters a name into the `txtUserName` control. If the `cmdCancel` button is pressed at this time, the `txtUserName` control and `txtPassword` will be blanked out.

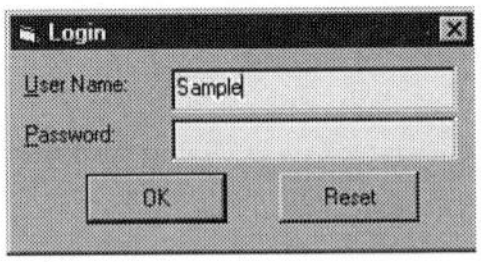

FIGURE **10.6**   The Cancel button has been renamed to provide additional functionality.

If the user entered SuperUser, the code would change the caption of the `cmdCancel` button and process the normal cancel code. This is shown in Figure 10.7.

FIGURE 10.7   The code for the Cancel button is controlled via
a Select Case code construct that determines what statements
are issued.

The examples in this lesson showed you how to use code to change and
retrieve the values of objects in your application during runtime. Although
the examples focused on the Login form and used the command button
object, these same principles can be applied to any other Visual Basic
objects that support property assignments during runtime.

SUMMARY

In this lesson, you learned how to set the properties of objects in your
application using the Properties dialog box. You also learned how to set,
retrieve, and base program operation of the current properties of objects in
your application. The examples gave you a glimpse into the power that
exists through dynamic property manipulation.

LESSON 11

DECLARING AND USING VARIABLES, CONSTANTS, AND DATA TYPES

In this lesson, you will learn how to define variables and constants in your program.

In Lesson 10 you learned what properties are and how to use them. Properties are memory locations that Visual Basic uses to store the information it needs to properly handle the different objects and commands in your application. In this chapter you will see how to define memory locations to be used by your program. These are called variables.

In addition, you will see how to define a constant. Constants eliminate the need to hard code values into the program code. The following line of code shows an example of hard coding values:

```
If sngSalesAmt > 50000 Then sngDiscount = .06
```

The problem with this is that when the test value or discount value changes, you must search the entire program for any references and change the code. Constants allow you to declare these values once and use the constant name anywhere in the program.

DEFINING A VARIABLE

Computer programs have the capability to work with and store information to be used in many different processes. This requires that the program can store and manipulate that information whenever it is needed. This is done using variables. A *variable* is a location in memory that you have given a name to. The name that you give to a variable can be almost any-thing, although there are some restrictions that will be discussed. You can declare a variable simply by using a name in the program, as shown in the following example. However, if `Option Explicit` is specified in the General Declarations, you must define every variable that you will use or an error will occur.

```
TotSales = 175000
```

The program can now refer to `TotSales` as if it were a number. Any math-ematical operation that can be done on a number can be done on a vari-able. The same is true for string variables as well. There are many different types of data that a variable can store depending on what type of process you are performing.

DATA TYPES

The different data types available to you represent the types of data that Visual Basic uses. Table 11.1 lists the different data types available in Visual Basic.

TABLE 11.1   VISUAL BASIC DATA TYPES

DATA TYPE	DESCRIPTION	DECLARATION CHARACTER	RANGE
Byte	1 Byte	None	0 to 255
Boolean	2 Bytes	None	True or False
Interger	2-byte integer	%	-32,768 to 32,768
Long	4-byte integer	&	-2,147,483,648 to 2,147,483,648
Single	4-byte floating-point number	!	-3.402823E38 to 3.402823E38
Double	8-byte floating-point number	#	1.797693134862 -32D308 to 1. .79769313486 232D308

continues

TABLE 11.1   CONTINUED

DATA TYPE	DESCRIPTION	DECLARATION CHARACTER	RANGE
Currency	8-byte number with fixed decimal	@	-922,337,203, 685,477.5808 to 922,337,203, 685,477.5808
Object	4 bytes	None	Any object reference
Date	8 bytes	None	1/1/100 to 12/31/9999
String	String of characters	$	0 through 65,500 characters
Variant	Date/Time floating-point numbers or strings	None	Can contain numeric data in the range as a double, or any string character

Any of these different data types can be declared as a variable. The default storage type for a variable is *Variant*. If you do not specify a data type, Variant will be used.

Variant is the most flexible type of variable that you can use. It can be used to work with most of the other data types, except for fixed-length strings. However, there are some problems with using the Variant data type. For example, you could have two Variant variables, one that is a string and the other that is a number. Visual Basic would let you try to multiply these two variables together because they are both Variants. Because they are different data types, an error would be displayed.

DECLARING VARIABLES

Declaring a variable is letting the program know that the variable exists and what type of data will be stored in it. As mentioned previously, you can name a variable almost anything, but there are some restrictions that are listed as follows:

* The name must begin with a letter (a–z, A–Z).

* The name can contain only letters, numbers, or the underscore character.

* It must not exceed 255 characters.

* It cannot be a Visual Basic reserved word. However, it can contain a reserved word (for example, OpenCustomer is valid, Open is invalid).

> **Tip**   When you name variables, try to use descriptive names. This will make your code much easier to maintain later in the process.

As you saw in Table 11.1, you can use a declaration character in the name of the variable to implicitly define the variable in the code, as shown in the following example:

```
OpenCustomer$ = "CustomerTable_One"
```

The first time Visual Basic processes this variable, it will declare it as a string variable. However, declaring variables in this way can cause many program errors and confusion. It is better to declare any variables in your program explicitly using a DIM statement.

DIMENSIONING VARIABLES

In order to declare or dimension a variable in the program, you would use the DIM statement. This informs the computer that you want to declare a variable. It also specifies the name and the data type of the new variable. Remember that if you omit the type, Variant will be assumed. The following is the syntax of the DIM statement:

```
Dim variable_name [As Variable_type]
```

The *variable_name* is the name that you decided to use for that variable. The *As Variable_name* is an optional parameter. The following example shows a routine in Visual Basic using the DIM statement:

```
Private Form_Load()
Dim Form_Loading As Boolean
Dim MsgBox_Title As String
Form_Loading = True
MsgBox_Title = "Demo of the DIM Statement"
MSGBOX "This is a Demo", vbOk, MsgBox_Title
End Sub
```

This code declares both variables prior to actually using them. By using this method, you will be reducing the amount of space that your program must use when executing. Another benefit of declaring variables this way is that Visual Basic will display any type mismatch error that might occur.

USING THE OPTION EXPLICIT STATEMENT

When dimensioning variables, there is one pitfall that you must watch out for. If you forget to declare a variable and then use it in your program, Visual Basic will implicitly declare it and you will never realize it. The same thing will happen if you misspell a variable; however, your program might not work correctly because there is now an extra variable being used that you are not aware of. To prevent this from happening, you should use the Option Explicit statement in the Declaration section of each form as shown in Figure 11.1.

FIGURE **11.1** Using the Declarations section to set the parameter.

The Option Explicit statement will instruct Visual Basic to display an error for any variable that was not explicitly dimensioned in the program. To ensure that you always have this setting turned on, you can set the option in Visual Basic so that every form or module you add to a project will automatically have this option added to it. You do this by selecting **Tools, Options** from the Visual Basic menu to display the Options dialog box (see Figure 11.2).

Tip   If you have Option Explicit set and DIM your variables in mixed case, when you type the variables as you code, the editor will change what you type to match the DIM. This will enable you to instantly spot when you have misspelled a variable.

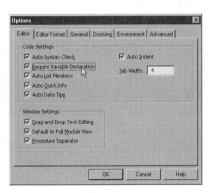

FIGURE **11.2**   Setting the Option Explicit statement as a global option.

By clicking the **Require Variable Declaration** setting, the Option Explicit statement will be included in every new form or module that you add to a project.

MODIFYING A VARIABLE

Constants are variables that cannot be modified within the program while it is executing. A constant, as the name implies, cannot be changed. If a value is needed in several different sections of code, it is recommended that you declare this value as a constant.

There are two main benefits of using a constant in your program. First, you do not have to remember a specific number to type into every section of code that uses it. You can declare a constant to be equal to that number and then use that constant wherever you would have referenced the number. The second benefit is the ability to change one value in the Declaration section of your program, and have all the references to it change automatically.

As an example, if you have a program that figures out sales tax and then prints a report, it is easy to just put the tax percentage directly into the program as a number. But, what happens if the tax percentage changes? You would have to look for every place in the program that you use the tax percentage and change it. By using a constant, you would change the constant value and the program would instantly use the new value. The syntax of a constant declaration follows:

```
Const variable_name [As variable_type] = value
```

Declaring a constant is similar to declaring a variable except for the assignment portion of the statement at the end of the declaration.

THE SCOPE OF A VARIABLE

The *scope* of a variable refers to how long it can be used and who (meaning which routines) can see it. There are three different types of scope a variable can have: global, module, and local. Although these might be slightly different concepts, let's look at each of them to see what they actually mean.

LOCAL SCOPE

Whenever you declare a variable inside a function, subroutine, or event routine, only the code within that procedure can see that variable. This is referred to as *local scope*. Listing 11.1 shows two routines with local variables defined in them.

LISTING 11.1   **LOCAL.TXT—DECLARING LOCAL VARIABLES WITH THE SAME NAMES**

```
Sub Routine1()
    Dim Var1 As Integer
    Dim Var2 As String
```

```
    Var1 = 6
    Var2 = "This is a Demo
End Sub
Sub Routine2()
    Dim Var1 As String
    Dim Var2 As Integer
    Var1 = "This is a Demo"
    Var2 = 85
End Sub
```

As you can see, the same variable names can be used in separate routines
because they are local to each routine and are not known by the other
routine.

MODULE SCOPE

The next type of scope is called *module*. You declare a variable with module scope by using the `Private` declaration statement. The syntax of the
`Private` statement is the same as a `DIM` statement except for the keyword
`Private`. Any variable declared as `Private` can be seen in any routine
within the module or form where it was declared. Listing 11.2 is the same
as the preceding example except it uses the term `Private` to define the
variables.

LISTING 11.2   **MODULE.TXT—DECLARING VARIABLES WITH MODULE**
SCOPE

```
Private Var1 As Integer
Private Var2 As String
Sub Routine1()
    Var1 = 6
    Var2 = "This is a Demo"
End Sub
Sub Routine2()
    Var2 = "This is a Demo"
    Var1 = 85
End Sub
```

You can see in this listing that by declaring the variables outside the routine, you cannot use the same variable name for different data types.

GLOBAL SCOPE

The last and most powerful of the scopes is *global scope*. To define a variable as global, you use the `Public` declaration statement. The syntax of

the Public statement is the same as a DIM statement except for the keyword Public. Any variable defined as Public can be used by any routine within the program.

> **Tip** Public variables can be defined only in the Declarations section of a code module. They cannot be declared with a form or routine.

Figure 11.3 shows the declaration of the variables used in the preceding example. After you have done this, you can use them in any routine, as shown in Listing 11.3.

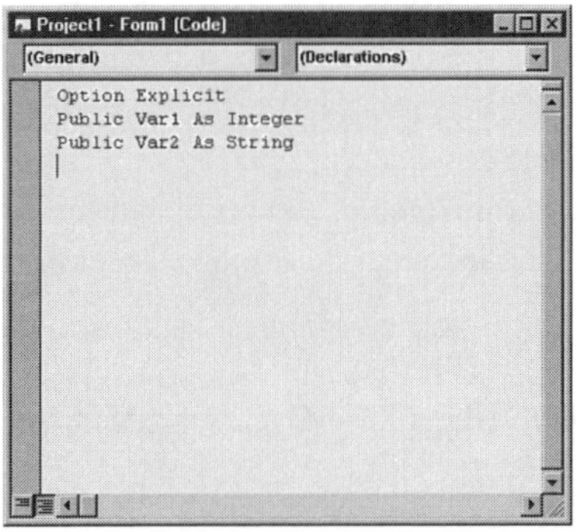

FIGURE 11.3   Declaring variables as Public in a project.

LISTING 11.3   GLOBAL.TXT—USING VARIABLES THAT ARE DEFINED AS Public

```
Sub Routine1()
    Var1 = 6
    Var2 = "This is a Demo"
End Sub
Sub Routine2()
    Var2 = "This is not a Demo"
    Var1 = 85
End Sub
```

Although you might think that Public variables are the best to use, you should know that when using Public variables it can be very easy to accidentally change the wrong variable in your program, which would cause a programming error to occur.

SHADOWING

There is one final issue to consider when naming variables within your program. Any variable that is declared with local scope that has the same name as a Public or Private variable will shadow the variable with the broader scope. Although this might sound confusing, it is really quite simple.

When two variables have the same name, the routine being executed will only see the variable that has the scope nearest to the routine. A variable with local scope overrides both Public and Private scope, while Private overrides Public scope. For example, if a variable named MyAddress was declared in a code module as Public, and within a subroutine a variable named MyAddress was also declared, the variable accessed in the subroutine will override the one that is declared in the code module.

SUMMARY

In this lesson you learned the difference between variables and constants. You learned what variables are, the different data types that you can use in your application, and how to declare them. You also learned how to use constants in your program to hold numbers or strings that will not change during the execution of the program. Finally, you learned the three types of scope in which a variable can be declared and how they affect the program as it executes.

In the next lesson, you will see how to control the flow of the program using various types of logic statements that are contained in Visual Basic.

LESSON 12

CONTROLLING PROGRAM FLOW

In this lesson, you learn how to make your program react to changing conditions by controlling the flow of the code.

When you begin designing an application, you will quickly realize that you need some way to control what sections of code are executed depending on the data being processed. This process is commonly referred to as *conditionally executing* the program code.

In order to execute certain sections of code conditionally, you must be able to respond to a condition or test. If the condition is true, then the code will be processed. This process is the basis of every program that has ever been written for a computer.

CONDITIONAL PROCESSING

Although there are many different ways to perform this test process, there is one primary way of doing it. The Visual Basic statement for performing these tasks is the `If...Then...End If` statement, or more commonly called the `If` statement.

If...Then...End If

If you haven't figured it out yet, the `If` statement works the way you would say it. In everyday speech, you might say, "If it rains, I will open an umbrella." In programming language, you would code, `If Rain = True Then Umbrella = "Yes"`. So that the `If` performs the test of the condition while the Then statement performs the action if the condition is met. The End If informs Visual Basic where the end of the condition code is. The following example illustrates how this works:

```
If OK_Cancel = 0 Then
        Exit Sub
End If
```

The condition OK_Cancel = 0 is tested to see whether it is true. If it is, the code between the Then and End If statements is executed. Otherwise, program execution would jump to the next statement following the End If. Conditional logic as shown in the preceding example is the mainstay of all but the simplest of Windows programs.

The conditional tests that you can use in an If statement can be as simple as the preceding example or as complex as the following:

```
If (keyascii < 48 Or keyascii > 58) And keyascii <> 8 Then
    Beep
    keyascii = 0
End If
```

Let's look at an example using the MsgBox function. When a MsgBox is used as a function, it returns a value that specifies which button was clicked. Listing 12.1 shows how to use it in conjunction with the If statement.

LISTING 12.1   IF_MSGBOX.TXT—USING THE If STATEMENT WITH THE MsgBox FUNCTION

```
Cancel = True
RC = MsgBox("Cannot Find Requested File! Continue?",
➥vbQuestion + vbYesNoCancel, "Demo App")
If RC = vbOK Then
    Cancel = False
    'Retry Find Process
End If
```

USING Else AND Else If

Even though the If statement is very powerful, it can test only one condition at a time. What do you do if you want to test for more than one condition? Luckily, there is a way to use the If statement to test for multiple conditions, as well as specify a default action if none of the conditions are true. There are two optional statements that you can use to extend the functionality of the If statement. The Else and Else If can be added to the If statement as shown in the following syntax:

```
If Condition Then
     [statements]
[Else If NextCondition Then
     [NextStatements]]
[Else
     [DefaultStatements]]
End If
```

As you can see, the Else If allows you to add one or more additional conditions to the statement. To specify a default action, you simply use the Else statement as the last statement in the If statement code block. Listing 12.2 adds these statements to the MsgBox example to show how it would work.

LISTING 12.2   ELSEIF.TXT—USING THE Else If AND Else STATEMENTS

```
Cancel = True
RC = MsgBox("Cannot Find Requested File! Continue?",
➡vbQuestion + vbYesNoCancel, "Demo App")
If RC = vbOK Then
     Cancel = False
     'Retry Find Process
Else If RC = vbNo Then
     Cancel = 0
     'Do not retry process
Else
     Cancel = 1
     'End program
End If
```

The way the If statement works is that the first condition is tested. If it is true, the related code in the Then statement is executed and the remaining If code is skipped. If it is not true, its related code block is skipped and the first Else If condition is tested. This process continues until either a condition is true or the Else statement block is executed. Place this code in the Form_Load event and try running the program to see what happens.

THE Select Case STATEMENT

Another method that can be used to perform conditional processing is the
Select Case statement. It is very useful when you must check a single
variable or expression for more than one value. Listing 12.3 shows how a
KeyDown event would check for a series of keys that might have been
pressed using an If...Then...Else code group.

**LISTING 12.3   IF_SELECT1.TXT—USING THE If STATEMENT TO TEST
FOR KEYSTROKES**

```
If KeyCode = vbKeyF1 Then
    'Process F1 code
ElseIf KeyCode = vbKeyF2 Then
    'Process F2 code
ElseIf KeyCode = vbKeyF3 Then
    'Process F3 code
ElseIf KeyCode = vbKeyF4 Then
    'Process F4 code
ElseIf KeyCode = vbKeyF5 Then
    'Process F5 code
ElseIf KeyCode = vbKeyF6 Then
    'Process F6 code
ElseIf KeyCode = vbKeyF7 Then
    'Process F7 code
Else
    'Process default code
End If
```

As you can see, this requires a good deal of typing. An easier way to perform these tests is with the Select Case statement. Using Select Case
you can specify the expression you want to test and then list all the possible cases or values that you want to respond to with a special action.
Listing 12.4 shows the same KeyDown process using the Select Case
statement.

**LISTING 12.4   IF_SELECT2.TXT—USING THE Select Case INSTEAD
OF THE If STATEMENT**

```
Select Case KeyDown
Case vbKeyF1
    'Process F1 code
Case vbKeyF2
    'Process F2 code
```

continues

LISTING 12.4   CONTINUED

```
Case vbKeyF3
     'Process F3 code
Case vbKeyF4
     'Process F4 code
Case vbKeyF5
     'Process F5 code
Case vbKeyF6
     'Process F6 code
Case vbKeyF7
     'Process F7 code
Case Else
     'Process default code
End If
```

If you compare both listings, you will quickly see that the Select Case is much easier to read.

> **Tip** Usually the Select Case should be used only when checking one expression for several possible values. If you must check multiple expressions, the If statement should be used.

DESIGNING LOOPS

When designing an application, you will quickly realize that much of the program processing that is done is repetitive. To perform these tasks, you would use one of the several forms of loop statements available in Visual Basic. A *loop* is a set of instructions that is executed repeatedly until some specific condition is satisfied. The following are the different loop statement groups that you can use:

- For...Next

- Do...While

- Do...Until

These three loop statements provide you with any type of loop process you might need in your program.

THE For...Next LOOP

This type of loop is called a counter-style loop process. It is done by incrementing a counter as part of the loop processing. The syntax of the For...Next statement is shown in the following example:

```
For Counter = Start to End [Step StepValue]
    [Statements]
Next [Counter]
```

Looking at the different parts of the For statement, you can see that the keyword For begins the loop process. The variable Counter contains the current iteration of the loop during its execution. The Start value represents the beginning value of the Counter, and End specifies the number at which point the loop will terminate. The optional parameter Step enables you to specify the value that is added to the counter after each iteration of the loop.

The final statement in the loop process is the Next statement, which informs Visual Basic that it should increment the counter and return to the top of the loop. This statement also checks to see whether the Counter value has reached or passed the End value specified; if it has, the loop will not be repeated and execution will continue to the next statement after the loop. Listing 12.5 shows a simple example of how the For...Next loop can be used in a program.

LISTING 12.5   FOR_NEXT.TXT—USING THE For...Next LOOP TO CHECK VALUES IN AN ARRAY

```
For I = 1 To 25
    If Array(I) = "NewYork" Then
        Msgbox "Found New York"
    End If
Next I
```

THE Step STATEMENT

The Step statement of the For...Next loop is optional. However, it can be useful depending on what you need a particular loop process to do. You do not have to define a step value when you write a For loop.

The following two statements are identical because of the default value of the Step parameter:

```
For I = 1 To 10
For I = 1 TO 10 Step 1
```

The Step statement enables you to skip over certain numbers or elements in an array by changing the value by which the counter is incremented.

Sometimes there will be a need to start at the largest value and work backward through an array or process. This is also done using the Step statement. By specifying a negative value for the step, the counter will be decreased by that value.

THE Exit For STATEMENT

For loops can be exited before the counter reaches the end point. By using the Exit For statement, you can leave the For loop at any point in the process, skipping over any code after the Exit For statement and resuming after the Next statement in the code. The Exit For statement is generally used in conjunction with some type of conditional code, such as the If statement. The code shown in Listing 12.6 is an example of the use of the Exit For statement.

LISTING **12.6**   **EXITFOR.TXT**—USING THE Exit For TO LEAVE A For LOOP

```
For I = 1 To 100
    If Array(I) = "NewYork" Then
        Msgbox "Found New York"
        Exit For
    End If
Next I
```

The code in listing 12.6 will exit the loop when the If condition is true. This prevents the code from looping more times than is needed.

> **Tip**   When using the For...Next loop, you should always specify the Counter variable in the Next statement to allow you to match the related For and Next statements, making maintenance easier.

THE Do While OR Do Until LOOP

Using the Do loop allows you to repeat code *while* or *until* a condition is met. For example, you might need a loop that searches for a specific value in an array and then ends when it is found. Listing 12.7 shows an example of this using the code from Listing 12.6.

LISTING 12.7   DO_WHILE.TXT—REPLACING THE For...Next STATEMENT WITH THE Do While

```
I = 1
Found = True
Do While(Found = True)
    If Array(I) = "NewYork" Then
        Found = False
    End If
    I = I + 1
Loop
```

As with the preceding code, this loop will continue until the specified string is found. The syntax of the Do loop statement is very similar to that of the For...Next statement and is shown here:

```
Do [{While ¦ Until} Condition]
    [Statements]
    [Exit Do]
Loop
```

Another way to code the same statement is by using a slightly different syntax as shown in the following statement:

```
Do
    [Statements]
    [Exit Do]
Loop [{While ¦ Until} Condition]
```

Although they might look almost the same, there is a remarkable difference between the way they work. The first version of the syntax requires that the condition be met for the loop to be executed at all. The second version of the syntax will allow the loop statements to be processed at least once even if the condition is not met. The placement of the condition specifies when and where the condition is tested.

A Do loop must consist of three parts. All loops must begin with the Do keyword and end with the Loop keyword. They must all have a third part as well, either the While or Until keyword.

The Do Until version of the Do loop is generally used to process code that reads data from a file or database. Listing 12.8 shows an example of a loop that reads data from a sequential file.

LISTING 12.8   DATAREAD.TXT—READING DATA FROM A FILE USING THE Do Until STATEMENT

```
Open "C:\cognos\bi97\user workspace\portdisplay.asc" For Input
As #1
I = 1
Do Until (EOF(1))
     Input #1, Region(I), MTD_Sales(I), YTD_Sales(I)
     I = I + 1
Loop
Total_Regions = I - 1
Close #1
```

As you can see in this listing, the condition that is being tested is a Visual Basic function that returns True when there is no more data to read from the file.

Loops provide you with a good way to perform repetitive tasks while reducing the amount of code you must write but not the program's functionality.

SUMMARY

This lesson has shown you several different ways to control the program's execution and flow of processing. Using the If...Then...End If loop or one of its variations allows you to test conditions and perform certain actions depending on the outcome of those tests. You have also seen a more advanced way to perform the same types of tests using the Select Case statement, which enables you to test a single expression many times without large amounts of repetitive code.

Besides testing conditions and acting on the results, you also learned how to perform repetitive tasks using the loop processing provided by Visual

Basic. This enables you to reduce the amount of code you must write and test for certain conditions at the same time.

Together, conditional processing and loop processing provide the backbone for your application and allow you to produce fairly complex procedures. In the next chapter, you will see how to use these concepts to enhance the actions of Windows events within your program.

LESSON 13

WORKING WITH FILES

In this lesson, you will learn how to create and access the contents of a file.

Almost every Windows application in existence today uses some type of file to hold data. Whether a program saves data into a database or just keeps information for its own use, most programs use files. The oldest and easiest ways to use files have been included in BASIC program languages since BASIC was around. Simple file access enables you to work with file data when there is no need of a larger database for your application.

In this chapter you will learn how to create a file, how to access it, and the different input and output procedures you will need to use. Three different types of file access are available:

- Sequential
- Random
- Binary

Each of these methods has its own good and bad points. Sequential access is probably the simplest file access you can use, but it can be slow and cumbersome to work with. Random file access is a much faster and useful method to access file data. However, using it is a bit more complex. Binary files are a special type of random access file that enable you to work with data a single byte or character at a time.

Random-access files, like random-access memory, can be accessed in any order. Random-access files will work with any kind of data that you define.

THE BASIC COMMANDS

Several Visual Basic commands are common to all forms of file input and output. The following list of commands will open the file, set the type of access, close the file, and check for an available number to assign to the file:

- Open

- Close

- FreeFile

- Print #

- Input #

- Write #

- Put #

- Get #

Depending on the file mode you are working with, you will use several of the preceding commands. The next few sections explain how the basic file processing works. The first and most important statement you need is the Open statement.

THE Open STATEMENT

The Open statement is used for all three types of file processing; the difference is in the parameters used in the statement. The Open statement starts a channel or path for reading or writing data to a file. The mode or file type the channel was opened for—either read, write, or both—dictates how the data can be accessed. The following is the syntax for the Open statement:

```
Open FileName [For Mode] [AccessRestriction] [LockType] As [#]
➥Channel% [Len = RecLength]
```

All Open statements must include the filename and file number, but the other parameters are optional. The file number is really another way of saying channel. The statement to open a text file might look like this:

```
Open "ReadMe.Txt" As #1
```

This will open the file named ReadMe.Txt and assign it file number 1. To reference this file in your program for either input or output, you would reference the file number. This file was opened in random-access mode because that is the default when the Mode parameter is omitted. Table 13.1 lists the different options for the Mode parameter.

TABLE 13.1   THE Open Mode SETTINGS

Mode	DESCRIPTION
Append	Opens a file for sequential output, beginning at the end of the file if it already exists. If the file does not exist, Visual Basic will create it. Append will never overwrite existing data in a file.
Binary	In Binary mode, you can access the data in a file at the byte level, meaning that you can write and read individual characters to and from the file.
Input	Opens a file for sequential input, starting at the beginning of the file. Data will be read in the same order that it was originally written to the file.
Output	Opens a file for sequential output, starting at the beginning of the file. If the file exists, Visual Basic will overwrite any data that was already there.
Random	Opens a file of random read and write access. This will allow data to be read from and written to a file at any specified record boundary.

Besides the Mode parameter, there are several other parameters that you might need when working with simple files:

- AccessRestriction

- LockType

- Len

Each of these will modify the actual access to the data in the file.

AccessRestriction

When the `AccessRestriction` parameter is specified in the `Open` statement, it will allow you to restrict the access of the file to Read, Write, or Read Write. These restrictions are often used when writing programs that will be used by more than one person at a time.

LockType

The `LockType` parameter is used to specify the operations permitted on the open file by other processes. You can restrict the access to a file so that only one user at a time has access to the file or can write to the file. This will prevent two users from making changes at the same time.

Len

The `Len` parameter is used to specify the length of the record that is used by random-access files that will be passed from Visual Basic to the file. This size is required when accessing records from a file. The first record in the file begins at location 1, and all other records are written at locations consecutively: record 2, 3, and so on.

THE `FreeFile` FUNCTION

You can open more than one file at a time as long as you assign a different file number to each new file you open. This requires you to keep track of the numbers that you have already used. To simplify this process, Visual Basic provides the `FreeFile` function, which can be used to request the next available file number from Visual Basic. By using this function, you are guaranteed that the file number you use is not being used elsewhere in the program. The following is the syntax for the `FreeFile` function:

```
IntFileNumber = FreeFile
Open "ReadMe.Txt" For Output As intFileNumber
```

Using the `FreeFile` function is recommended whenever you are going to access more than one file at a time so that a problem does not happen.

> **Tip** You should not use the `FreeFile` function directly in the `Open` statement as shown:
>
> ```
> Open "ReadMe.Txt" For Output As FreeFile
> ```
>
> This prevents you from knowing what the new file number is that was just assigned. To access the file later in the program, you must know what the number is.

THE `Close` STATEMENT

After you open the file, you will eventually need to close it. Although Visual Basic will close all open files for you, closing them in your program code is good programming practice. This will prevent any unexpected data errors from happening. The statement to close a file is `Close`. This statement takes the open file number as its parameter, as shown in the following example:

```
Close intFileNumber
or
Close #1
```

The second version of the statement assumes that the file you are closing was opened as #1. You can specify any number of files to close in a single `Close` statement. In fact, if you do not specify a file number, Visual Basic will close all the open files. This is very useful when the program is terminating due to an error; you can at least close all the files normally.

CREATING THE FILE ACCESS CODE

Although nothing will actually happen yet, you can create the initial file access routine using the code shown in Listing 13.1. One of the tricks you should notice in this code is the use of a variable to specify the file to open. This enables you to set or modify the filename once in the program without having to search for all the references to it.

LISTING **13.1**   USING THE **Open** AND **Close** STATEMENTS TO ACCESS A
FILE

```
Dim intFileNumIn As Integer
Dim intFileNumOut As Integer
Dim InputFile As String
Dim OutputFile As String

'Set the input and output file names
InputFile = "CheckProcess.Dat"
OutputFile = "CancelledChecks.Dat"

 'Open the Input File
 intFileNumIn = FreeFile      'Get an available file number
Open InputFile For Input As intFileNumIn

 'Open the Output File
 intFileNumOut = FreeFile       'Get an available file number
Open OutputFile For Output As intFileNumOut
 '
 '
 'Insert the Program processing code here!
 '
 '
 '
Close intFileNumIn
Close intFileNumOut
```

ACCESSING SEQUENTIAL FILES

Sequential file access means exactly what it says, everything happens
sequentially. When you create a sequential file, you are creating a file that
must be read from and written to from the beginning to the end. This is
the biggest fault in sequential processing. Most applications require access
to a given piece of information no matter where it actually is on the file.
With sequential files, you must process the entire file even if you need
only a few bytes of information toward the end of the file. The two main
statements that are used when working with a sequential file are the Print
and Input statements.

THE `Print` STATEMENT

After you open a file, you must put information into it. One common approach is the `Print` statement. `Print #` writes only to a sequential-access type file using the following syntax:

```
Print #intFileNum, [OutputList]
```

The `Outputlist` can consist of one or more of the functions listed in Table 13.2.

TABLE 13.2   THE `Print #` STATEMENT COMPONENTS

FUNCTION	DESCRIPTION
Spc(number)	Used to insert *number* of spaces into the output.
Tab(number)	Used to position the insertion point to an absolute column number represented by *number.* Without a number specified, `Tab` will position the data at the beginning of the next print zone.
Expression	A numeric or string expression that contains the data you want to write to the file.
CharPos	Specifies the insertion point for the next character to print.

To see how this works, start a new project and add the following code to the `Click` event of a command button on the form. Then, run the program to create and add the data to the file. When the program ends, use Notepad to open the file you created to see the information that was written (see Figure 13.1).

```
Dim intFileNumOut As Integer
Dim OutputFile As String
Dim intCtr As Integer

'Set the input and output file names
OutputFile = "c:\PrintDemo.Txt"
```

```
'Open the Output File
intFileNumOut = FreeFile       'Get an available file number
Open OutputFile For Output As intFileNumOut
'

For intCtr = 1 to 10
     Print # intFileNumOut, intCtr
Next intCtr
   '

Close intFileNumOut
```

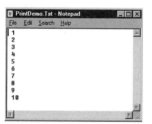

FIGURE **13.1**   Displaying the data that was written to the file.

THE **Write** STATEMENT

The Write statement is another command that can be used to write information to a sequential file. The only difference between the Print and
Write statements is that all the data that the Write statement writes to a
file is comma-delimited, not space-delimited as with the Print statement.
In addition, by using the semicolon after a variable in the Write statement, the next value will be written to the same line instead of to the next
line of the file. To see how this works, change the statement

```
Print # intFileNumOut, intCtr
```

to

```
Write # intFileNumOut, intCtr;
```

And then re-execute the program. When you look at the data in Notepad
this time, it should all be on one line, as shown in Figure 13.2.

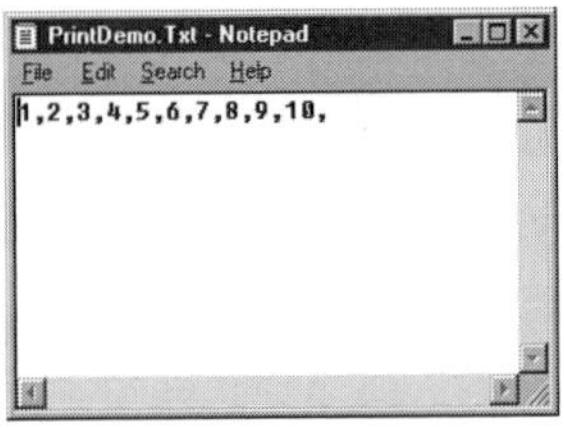

FIGURE 13.2   Using the Write statement to output data.

THE Input STATEMENT

After the data is written, reading back the data often takes place in a separate procedure or in another application that needs the data. To read the
data from a sequential file, you must use the Input statement, which is
used to read data from a sequential file. You must read the data in exactly
the same order and format as you wrote it, due to the nature of sequential
file processing. The syntax of the Input statement resembles the Print or
Write statement and is shown in the following example:

```
Input # intFileNum, variable1 [,variable2][, …variableN]
```

The Input statement requires an open file number and variables to hold
the data you are reading. The following code reads the data from the file
you created in the previous section and displays it in a MsgBox:

```
Dim intFileNumIn As Integer
Dim InputFile As String
Dim intCtr As Integer
Dim intData As Integer

'Set the input and output file names
InputFile = "c:\PrintDemo.Txt"

'Open the Input File
intFileNumIn = FreeFile      'Get an available file number
Open InputFile For Input As intFileNumIn
'
For intCtr = 1 to 10
     Input # intFileNumIn, intData
     MSGBOX "The Number is: " & CSTR(intData)
Next intCtr
 '
Close intFileNumIn
```

The Input statement is a fairly simple statement because it performs the mirror image task of the Print. Try adding the preceding code to another command button in the program and execute it to see what happens.

> **Plain English**   The CStr function used in the preceding code will convert the number specified as the argument into a string.

USING RANDOM-ACCESS FILES

Whereas sequential files require you to process the entire file to find the data you need, random-access files enable you to read and write the data in any order. For example, you can write order records to a random-access file and then read one or more order records later in any order you need them. If the order file was sequential, you would have to read every record in the file that preceded the ones you wanted. If you don't specify the file mode to be used when the Open statement is executed, the file will be opened in random-access mode. Besides this small difference, the Open and Close statements work exactly the same as with sequential files.

The big difference is in the processing. Suppose you have a file with 20 records in it and you need to access the 12th record. In sequential mode, you would need to read the first 11 records to get to the 12th. Then, you would have to read the last eight records to complete the read process. If you use random access, you could go directly to the 12th record.

The same is true when you want to write data to the file. If you want to change the 10th record of the file, you would have to read all the records in the file, change the 10th record, and write all the records back to the file. In random mode, you would only need to read, change, and then write the 10th record.

When dealing with a small file this might be no big deal, but if you are working with a file that contains 10,000 records it becomes a concern.

THE Get AND Put STATEMENTS

When working in random-access mode, the two statements you will use to read and write data to the file are the Get and Put statements. These statements are similar to the Print and Input statements you used for sequential processing. The major difference between them is that the Print and Input statements handle one piece of data at a time and must go through the entire file when they are used.

The syntax for the Put and Get statements shows the difference immediately. These statements require a record number to write to or retrieve.

```
Put intFileNum, [intRecordNum,] Variable
Get intFileNum, [intRecordNum,] Variable
```

By specifying the record number you want to work with, you can update or read only certain data. The variable that you read or write can be any data type, including an array or a user-defined variable. The freedom to handle any type of variable as a single unit is one of the most powerful features of the random-access file. To see how this works, use the same file you created earlier to read only a specified record from the file. The following code will read a single record and display the value using a MsgBox:

```
Dim intFileNumIn As Integer
Dim InputFile As String
Dim intRecordNum As Integer
Dim intData As Integer

'Set the input and output file names
InputFile = "c:\PrintDemo.Txt"

'Open the Input File
intFileNumIn = FreeFile      'Get an available file number
Open InputFile For Random As intFileNumIn
'
intRecordNum = 6
Get # intFileNumIn, intRecordNum, intData
MSGBOX "The Number is: " & CSTR(intData)
'
Close intFileNumIn
```

Summary

In this lesson, you have seen the different statements that are related to creating and using simple files. This included the different file modes and access methods that you could use. You have seen how both sequential and random-access files work and learned that random-access files are used more often than sequential files in an application that contains large amounts of data. In Lesson 14, "Connecting to the Database," you are going to see how to access data that is contained in a database using the Visual Basic commands and controls.

LESSON 14

CONNECTING TO THE DATABASE

In this lesson, you will get an understanding of what a database is and how to use it from your application.

In Lesson 13, "Working with Files," you learned how to access data in simple files that exist on your computer. Although this type of file access is useful for very small applications, most business applications use something called a database. A database provides a method of controlling the data that is entered into your application without having to create all the routines and functions needed to perform the actual interaction with the database. In this chapter, you will get an understanding of what a database really is, the terms used when discussing a database, and how to use it from a Visual Basic application.

A BRIEF INTRODUCTION

Data is the information that your application uses to perform the tasks for which it was created. Everything that you come into contact with contains data. For example, if you collect baseball cards, you might keep track of the players' names, dates, averages, and card values. In any business, certain information about customers, products, prices, financial status, and so on must be saved. All this information is called *data*. When you organize this data in a meaningful way, it becomes information. The best way to organize this data is by using something called a relational database management system (RDBMS). This is a fancy way to describe a database.

A database basically does three things:

- Lets you store data in it
- Keeps the data
- Allows you to access the data when needed

The first collections of data were done using simple files, like the ones described in Chapter 13. However, as the amount of data and the types of processing done on it have increased, databases have become separate applications that run on the computer and deliver the data to other applications when requested. Many different databases are available for you to use in your application. The most common of these include

- Microsoft Access

- Microsoft FoxPro

- Oracle Personal 7

- Sybase SQL Anywhere

These database applications are examples of *local* databases, those that run on your computer. However, these databases are just too small to use for very large or complex applications. For these applications, you would use one of several server or remote databases, which include

- Oracle

- Sybase

- DB2

These databases actually run on separate, more powerful computers called servers. Your application would connect to that server and request data from that database. Visual Basic works well with either type of database and provides the tools to access the data easily.

TERMS AND CONCEPTS

Learning to use a database can be a frightening exercise. However, after you understand the terms that are used with a database it becomes a bit easier to follow. A database is made up of several objects that are listed and explained in Table 14.1.

TABLE 14.1   DATABASE TERMS

TERM	DESCRIPTION
Column	The smallest piece of information in a database. A column can be thought of as a single field of data, such as a phone number or a city.
Row	A row contains all the columns for a single related item. An example would be a row of data that contains the name, address, and phone number for an address book.
Table	A collection of rows that are related to each other by a common idea, such as the Customer table, which contains all the information about the customers.
Join	A join describes how one table is related to, or connects with, another. How the Customer table relates to the Orders table is defined as a join.
SQL	Structured Query Language (SQL) is the special language used to access the data contained in a database.

Everything that affects a database is controlled by the database engine or application for that database. In addition to Visual Basic, you would use another computer language call SQL to access the data in the database. SQL was created specifically to interact with a database engine and is common across almost every database you might use.

ADVANTAGES OF USING A DATABASE

You might be thinking, "What's the big deal about a database"? Although it is true that you can use simple files to store the data for your application and relate them together yourself, you should look at the effort you would need to put into it before choosing this path. In order to use simple files instead of a database, you would need to design and code the following routines:

- Insert data column

- Delete data column

- Update data column

- Verify routine to check for valid data in each unique column

This might not seem diffcult. However, if you think about it a little, you will realize that for every table (file) and every field (column) you would need a separate routine to perform these actions. If your application contains many tables, which themselves contain many columns, you can see how this gets complicated very quickly.

Using a database to control all these actions allows you to concentrate on what your application is going to do instead of how to access the data. This also reduces the amount of code that you must write and maintain in your application. Visual Basic makes it even easier to access databases by providing several data controls and objects that assist you in the access process.

RETRIEVING DATA

Three unique controls can be used in Visual Basic to access a database. They are described in Table 14.2.

TABLE 14.2   DATA ACCESS CONTROLS

CONTROL	DESCRIPTION
Data control	Used to access any simple database, such as Access or dBASE
Remote data control	Used together with an ODBC connection to access any database available
ActiveX data control	The newest data control, it uses the new OLEDB connections to access any database available

For the purpose of this chapter, you will see how to use the standard Data control to access the information in a sample database that comes with Visual Basic. In addition, you will see how to work with other controls in Visual Basic that can interact with the Data control to display the information to the user.

CONNECTING THE DATABASE

The Data control is the main support to a very sophisticated access method that you can use to access the database from your application. By setting only a few properties of the Data control, you can connect to the database and retrieve information from it. This is all done without writing a single line of Visual Basic code. To actually use the Data control on a form, you must perform three easy steps:

1. Place the Data control on the form.

2. Set the DatabaseName property to the database you want to access.

3. Set the RecordSource property to the table or SQL query from which you want to retrieve data.

To see how this works, start a new project in Visual Basic and place the Data control on the form. Then, set the DatabaseName property to the Access database, Biblio.mdb, that comes with Visual Basic (see Figure 14.1).

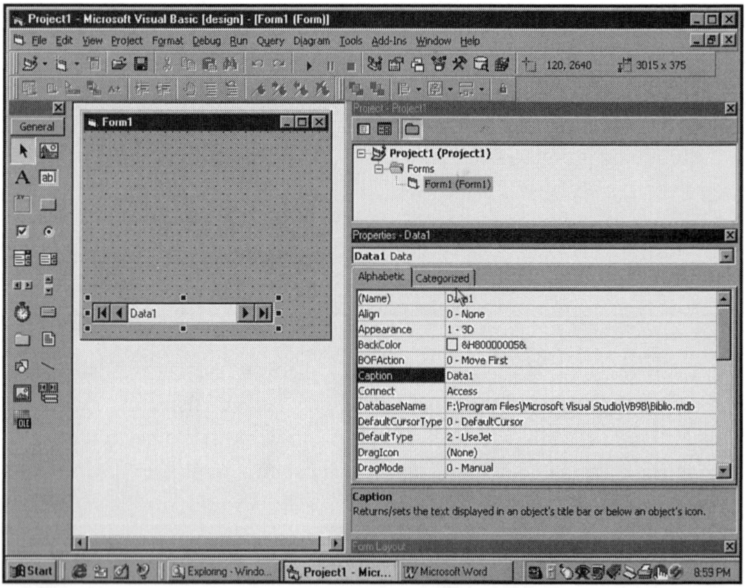

FIGURE 14.1   Specifying the database for the Data control to connect to.

Next, assign the recordset property to the Authors table contained in the database, as shown in Figure 14.2.

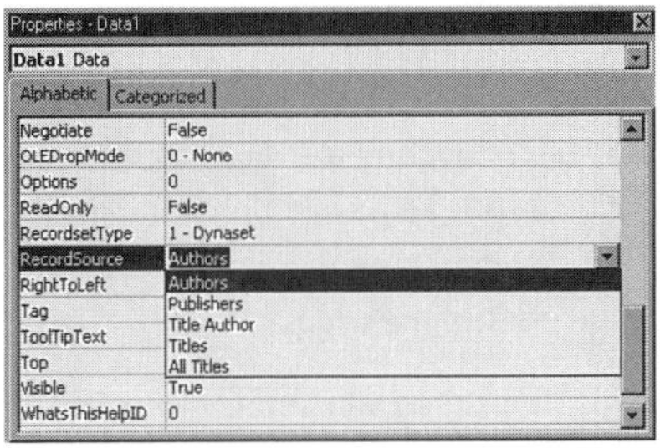

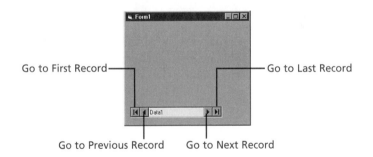

FIGURE 14.2   Selecting the table to access.

When you execute this application, other than the Data control, there would be nothing else displayed on the form (see Figure 14.3). The Data control also provides a set of navigation functions that users and the application can access to select data. With these buttons, users can move to the first, last, next, or previous row in the recordset. The button design is similar to the buttons you would find at home on a VCR.

Go to First Record ⎯⎯⎯⎯   ⎯⎯⎯⎯ Go to Last Record

Go to Previous Record   Go to Next Record

FIGURE 14.3   Placing the Data control on the form.

As you can see, the Data control has a lot of capabilities for you to use. However, by itself, it does not do very much. You must add other controls to the form before it will really work.

DISPLAYING THE DATA

The next step in the process of working with database information is to display the data from the recordset that is retrieved. Again, Visual Basic and the Data control provide an easy way to perform these tasks. Most of the controls that are available in Visual Basic are known as data-aware controls. The process of connecting a control to the Data control is called *binding* it to the Data control. To have a bound control work, you must set only a few properties, depending on the control. Most bound controls use two main properties to control the access:

- DataSource—Defines the Data control to which it is attached. There can be more than one Data control on a form.

- DataField—Specifies the column in the recordset to be retrieved.

To see how this all works, add two text boxes to the form you created earlier, as shown in Figure 14.4.

FIGURE **14.4**   Adding two bound controls to display the data in the Data control.

Set the DataSource property of the first text box. Next, you must specify which column the text box will display by setting the DataField property. For this example, select Data1 and Author as shown in Figure 14.5. Select another field from the Authors table for the second text box.

Now, run the application again. You should see that data is now being displayed in the controls that you've added to the form (see Figure 14.6). Try using the navigation buttons on the Data control to move around the recordset. As you can see, you are accessing the data in the Authors table without writing any code.

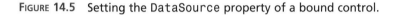

FIGURE **14.5**   Setting the `DataSource` property of a bound control.

FIGURE **14.6**   Displaying the data from the database without writing any code.

As simple as this application is, you can even change the data shown in the text boxes to update the database. This is possible because the Data control will issue an `Update` command to the database whenever you move to another row in the recordset. However, in most database applications, you will need to perform more complicated processing than can be performed by the Data control itself.

ACCESSING THE DATA CONTROL IN CODE

Although the Data control is a very powerful tool when it comes to accessing a database, there will be times when you must write code to perform more complex functions or editing with the data. Fortunately, you can use the Data Access Objects commands in conjunction with the Data control recordset to manipulate the data in the code. Like any other object in Visual Basic, the Data control contains many events and methods that you can use to access the data using program commands. You will use the following events most often:

- Validate—This event is executed whenever a navigation button is processed or when the form closes.

- Error—This event is triggered whenever there is an error during an automated process of the Data control.

- Reposition—This event is executed whenever the current record is changed.

By using these events in conjunction with Data Access commands, you can perform almost any task with the database and Data control. The following is an example of using the Validate event:

```
Private Sub Data1_Validate(Action As Integer, Save As Integer)
    If Not IsDate(txtDate.Text) Then
            MsgBox "The Authors Birthdate is Invalid" & _
                vbCRLF & "Please Re-enter!", vbCritical,
                ➡App.Title
            Action = vbDataActionCancel
            txtDate.DataChanged = False
            txtDate.Text = "??/??/??"
        End If
    End If
End Sub
```

This code checks the Save parameter to see whether any of the data in the bound text box control has been changed. If there have been changes, the txtDate.Text value is checked to see whether it contains a valid date. If is doesn't, the Action parameter is used to cancel the update and a message is displayed to the user explaining the error. Besides using the Data control events, you can also add code that manipulates the data with the Data control when a user clicks a command button or another action takes place in the application. A good example of this process is to add the code to delete a row from the recordset attached to the Data control. First, add two command buttons to the form as shown in Figure 14.7.

Then, add the code shown in Listing 14.1 to each command button's Click event.

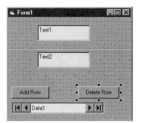

FIGURE 14.7   Adding additional commands to the data access form.

LISTING 14.1   DELETING A ROW FROM THE RECORDSET USING THE DATA
CONTROL

```
Private Sub cmdAddRecord_Click()
'Command to add a new record,
'place in click event of Add button
    data1.Recordset.AddNew
End Sub

Private Sub cmdDeleteRecord_Click()
'Commands to delete a record,
'placed in click event of Delete button
    data1.Recordset.Delete
    If Not data1.EOF Then
        data1.Recordset.MoveNext
    Else
        data1.Recordset.MoveLast
    End If
End Sub
```

To see how this code works, run the application and click the command
button to delete a row. This routine uses several of the available methods
of the Data control's recordset object.

SUMMARY

In this lesson you took a quick look at a very useful set of tools, functions, and commands that you can use to access information in a database.
Using the Data control gives you quick access to the database without
writing large amounts of code. However, in most complex database applications, you will need to understand more about the Data Access objects,
which provide complete programmed access to the database, as well as
SQL programming to create complex queries that manipulate the data
before your application accesses it.

Lesson 15
The Common Dialog Control

Dialog boxes let your applications interact with users by using the same forms that Windows uses. Today's lesson introduces you to the different options available in the Windows Common Dialog control and how to use it.

What the Common Dialog Is All About

When the old DOS-based computers changed from black-and-white to color displays, many new commands had to be created for users to change these new properties. Then, when Windows was introduced, developers knew that users would perform many activities over and over. The outcome of this knowledge led to the creation of a "set" of Windows dialog boxes that interfaced with users.

When Microsoft started producing developer tools such as Visual Basic for the Windows environment, the company created a special tool—the Common Dialog control, which has been included with every version of Visual Basic. The Common Dialog control provides a standard set of dialog boxes for functions such as opening and saving files, setting print options, and changing colors and fonts. The control can also display help through the Windows help engine.

Adding the Common Dialog Control

The actual common dialog routines are distributed in a dynamic link library file called COMDLG32.DLL. The way in which you, as the developer, interact with this library is by using the Common Dialog control. Although this control is used in almost every application that you may create, it's not one of the default controls displayed in the Visual Basic toolbox. You must add it by selecting **Project, Components** (or pressing Ctrl+T). Select **Microsoft Common Dialog Control 6.0**, as shown in Figure 15.1.

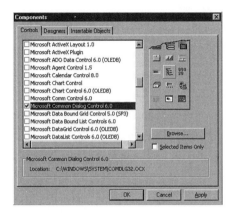

FIGURE 15.1   Adding the Common Dialog control to the toolbox.

Notice the filename of the control at the bottom of the screen. The Common Dialog control is contained in the file COMDLG32.OCX.

As a review, the Common Dialog control can access five standard Windows dialog boxes and one function:

- Open/Save As enables users to select files to open or choose filenames to save.

- Font lets users choose a base font and set any font attributes they want.

- Color allows users to choose from a standard color or create a custom color for use in the program.

- Print lets users select a printer and set some of the printer parameters.

- Help accesses the Windows help engine to display the referenced help file.

USING THE COMMON DIALOG CONTROL

Now that you've added the control to your toolbox, you can use it on any form in a project. You will see the control on the form in Design mode, and you can change the properties of it and use different methods on it. However, you don't see it on the form at runtime. When your program calls for one of the Common Dialog control's various forms, Visual Basic displays the form and handles the appropriate actions before passing control back to you. Figure 15.2 shows the Common Dialog control on the toolbox and on the form.

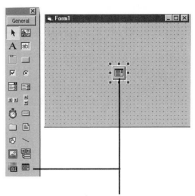

The Common Dialog control

FIGURE 15.2   The Common Dialog control.

To use any of the different functions, you must set some of the control's properties by using the Properties window or the Common Dialog control's Property Pages dialog box (see Figure 15.3). The Property Pages dialog box provides an easy way to access the specific properties needed for each Common Dialog type. To access the Property Pages dialog box, right-click the control and select **Properties** from the pop-up menu. Because you need only one control to access any of the different functions available, you can set the properties for all of them at the same time.

Setting these properties determines which dialog box will appear when called for. This does not initiate the dialog box, however. The dialog box will appear only when called upon by your code to do so. You determine which dialog box appears by setting the control's properties and executing a method that tells the control to create the dialog box with your settings.

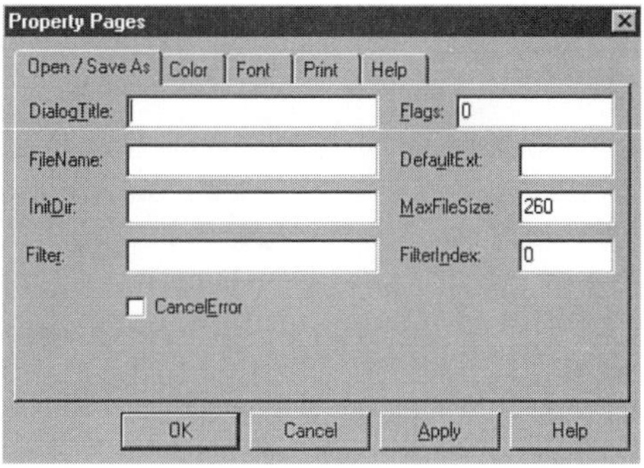

FIGURE 15.3   The Property Pages for the Common Dialog control enables you to change many of the control's properties.

Besides the properties that you can set at design time, you must use one of the following methods to produce the dialog box you require. Table 15.1 lists the methods used to open each dialog box type and explains how each dialog box is used.

TABLE 15.1   ACTION METHODS FOR THE COMMON DIALOG BOXES

DIALOG TYPE	METHOD	DESCRIPTION
Color Selection	ShowColor	Displays a dialog box in which users select from a palette of colors or customize color selections.
Font Selection	ShowFont	Displays a dialog box in which users can select from available font sizes and styles.
WinHelp	ShowHelp	Calls the Windows Help engine and displays a dialog box in which the user can select from the help you've provided.

continues

TABLE 15.1   CONTINUED

DIALOG TYPE	METHOD	DESCRIPTION
Open File	ShowOpen	Displays a dialog box in which users can select a file as well as navigate among various drives, folders, and wildcards to select the file.
Printer Selection	ShowPrinter	Displays a dialog box in which the user can select a printer and set print settings.
Save File	ShowSave	Displays a dialog box in which the user can specify which filename to save to.

Using these methods makes the resulting code not only more precise, but also makes it very easy to understand.

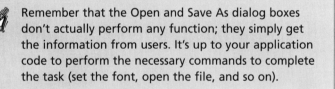

Remember that the Open and Save As dialog boxes don't actually perform any function; they simply get the information from users. It's up to your application code to perform the necessary commands to complete the task (set the font, open the file, and so on).

THE COLOR DIALOG BOX

Today's PC can produce a large variety of colors. The Color dialog box gives users a standard way to select a color to use. With a Common Dialog control named cdlColor1 on your form, the following code would produce Figure 15.4:

```
cdlColor1.ShowColor
```

After selecting a color to use, you can use the value returned to you from the dialog box control as follows:

```
txtTest1.ForeColor=cdlColor1.Color
```

FIGURE 15.4   The Color selection common dialog box.

This sets the foreground color of the text in `txtTest1` to the hexadecimal value found in `cdlColor1.Color`. The color property doesn't understand red; it only knows how to deal with the hexadecimal representation of the color red.

You could also set some flag property settings before calling the control. The following code produces Figure 15.5:

```
cdlColor1.Flags=cdlCCFullOpen
```

This tells the controls to default to opening the Define Custom Colors section of the control.

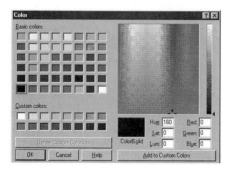

FIGURE 15.5   The Color selection common dialog box with a color definition section.

THE FONT DIALOG BOX

You use the Font dialog box to prompt the user for a font to use. The dialog box lists the installed fonts and their available style settings for selection. As you did when using the Color dialog box, you can set various flags to tell the control how to behave. The Font control is slightly different in that you must set at least one of three flag properties before the Font dialog box will appear without error. This value is either cdlCFScreenFonts, cdlCFPrinterFonts, or cdlCFBoth. This tells Visual Basic whether you want to select from available screen fonts, printer fonts, or both. The following code displays the Font dialog box shown in Figure 15.6.

```
cdlDialog1.Flags=cdlCFScreenFonts   'Displays only screen fonts
cdlDialog1.ShowFont
```

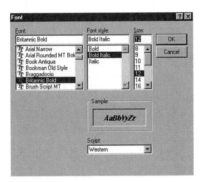

FIGURE 15.6   The Font selection common dialog box.

> Tip   By searching the Help subsystem on the keyword Flags, you will locate the full list of available Common Dialog control flag settings.

THE FILE OPEN/SAVE AS DIALOG BOX

The File Open/Save As dialog box is probably one of the most commonly used sets of dialog boxes you'll run into. It contains controls to let you

navigate to other folders or drives. This dialog box has some important
settings that you can use to narrow its display. The following uses some of
these settings to display the dialog box shown in Figure 15.7:

```
cdlDialog1.Flags=cdlOFNHelpButton + cdlOFNLongNames
cdlDialog1.Filter= "Text Files¦*.txt¦ Word Docs¦*.doc"
cdlDialog1.ShowOpen
```

FIGURE 15.7   A File Open dialog box showing Word documents.

When you work with any of the Common Dialog control's different functions, you use several properties to set up the interface. In the case of the
Open/Save As dialog boxes, these properties are as follows:

- Filter—Sets the file-extension filters displayed in the Type
  list box.

- FilterIndex—Contains the default filter for the Open and Save
  As dialog boxes.

- Flags—Sets the options for the dialog boxes.

- Filename—Contains the path and filename of a selected file.

- DefaultExt—Used as the extension when a file with no
  extension is saved.

- InitDir—Sets the initial file directory that's displayed.

- MaxFileSize—Indicates the maximum string size of the data in
  the Filename property.

The only two properties that require more than one or two lines to explain are `Filter` and `Flags`. The `Filter` property provides users with a list of filters to choose from. The pipe (¦) is used to separate the description and the filter values from each other. The following is an example of the syntax for setting the `Filter` property:

```
Text (*.txt)¦*.txt¦Word Documents (*.doc)¦¦*.doc¦Any Files¦*.*
```

 Tip Don't use any spaces before or after the pipe symbol. Any spaces would be displayed with the description and filter values.

This example also allows users to display any file type by selecting the Any Files filter type.

You can change many different settings for the `Flags` property. The following are used in this sample application:

- `cdlOFNFileMustExist`—If this flag is set for the Open dialog box, users can select only files that exist.

- `cdlOFNOverwritePrompt`—This causes the Save As dialog box to confirm an overwrite of an existing file.

THE PRINT DIALOG BOX

The Print dialog box departs a little from the direct interaction with the visible properties that users can modify by using the Common Dialog control. This dialog box is usually displayed just before your application sends data to the printer. It enables users to choose which printer to use and also to set the options for the print process. The command `cdlDialog1.ShowPrinter` produces the dialog box shown in Figure 15.8.

As in the other dialog boxes, the Print dialog box doesn't actually send anything to your printer; you must code the correct set of Visual Basic statements to perform that task. The following code example shows how the Printer dialog box can be used to set the current printer's options:

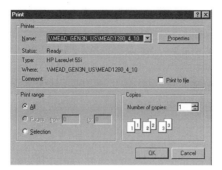

FIGURE 15.8   The Print dialog box lets users set printer options by using a consistent interface.

```
Private Sub cmdPrint_Click()
Dim FileCopies As Integer
    Dim StartPage As Integer
    Dim EndPage As Integer

    dlgFileSelect.Flags = cdlPDPrintToFile Or cdlPDCollate
    dlgFileSelect.ShowPrinter

' If this statement is true, you would need to display the
' Save As dialog box in order for the user to specify the
' name of the new saved file.

    If dlgFileSelect.Flags And cdlPDPrintToFile =
    cdlPDPrintToFile Then
        MsgBox "This text will be printed to a file"
    End If

' Set the nuber of copies and from/to page values before going
' to the printer.
    StartPage = dlgFileSelect.FromPage
    EndPage = dlgFileSelect.ToPage
    FileCopies = dlgFileSelect.Copies
End Sub
```

Again, you can see that the actual call to the Common Dialog control remains pretty much the same. When you must see whether a particular value was set in the Flags property, you would use the Boolean AND function, as shown in the preceding If statement code. Also, the properties for the number of copies and the pages to print are saved in variables. You would need to use them as counters in loops or pass them to the reporting tool that will actually do the printing process for you. If you run your application and click the **Print** button, you will see how the interaction with the Print dialog box and the related Printer Setup dialog box allows your application to have the integrated Windows feel to it.

DISPLAYING HELP

You can display a help file to your user in two different ways:

- By using the help engine API functions, which requires you to define the functions and to understand how to use them

- By using the Help dialog box accessible from the Common Dialog control—a much easier method

To use this dialog box properly, you must set the help-related properties to point to a formatted Windows help file (.HLP).

- HelpFile specifies the path and filename of a Windows help file.

- HelpCommand sets the type of help display requested.

The HelpCommand setting that you'd normally use is cdlHelpContents, which tells the help engine to display the contents topic in the specified help file. To see how this works, add one last command button to the form in the open project, and then insert the following code in its Click event routine:

```
' Set the name of the help file
    dlgFileSelect.HelpFile = "c:\program files\Microsoft
    ➥Visual Studio\Common\Tools\Reports\crw.HLP"
    dlgFileSelect.HelpCommand = cdlHelpContents
' Display Visual Basic Help contents topic.
    dlgFileSelect.ShowHelp
```

This code displays the Contents page for the Crystal Reports help file that comes with Visual Basic. When it's displayed, users are in the standard Windows 95 help application and can navigate to any area of the help file that they need to go.

SUMMARY

In this lesson, you learned how to use the Common Dialog control to interact with the user in real-world situations. Each different dialog box lets you allow users to control the look of the application. It also gives them the control to modify the printer options when printing from your application. The Open and Save As dialog boxes let users specify which files they want to use when working with the application.

LESSON 16

USING THE PRINT FEATURES

In this lesson, you will learn how to use the built-in print features of Visual Basic, how to access the Printer *object to control printing, and how to select the printer to use.*

 Caution Visual Basic's printer interface is not as simple as some of the other components that you have already seen. In many instances, printing data from a Visual Basic application is not a trivial task.

PRINTING APPLICATION FORMS

Depending on the application, you might need to print the image of the form that is currently displayed to the user. Visual Basic includes the PrintForm method that applies to any form within your project. When you issue a PrintForm method, Visual Basic begins printing the form immediately. So, if you are building or drawing the form for the user, the process should be completed before you issue the PrintForm method. The PrintForm method does not really suffice for most of your printing needs, but the method works well for outputting a complete form to the printer. Perhaps the best benefit of PrintForm, as well as the other supported printer-output capabilities, is that Visual Basic uses Windows printer objects. This means you never have to worry about specifying the printing instructions that are unique to a certain printer.

THE `PrintForm` METHOD

Using the `PrintForm` method is as simple as specifying the form name and the method, as shown in the following syntax:

```
[frmForm].PrintForm
```

Notice that `frmForm` is optional. If the form name is not specified, the `PrintForm` method will reference the current form. To print a form named `frmWelcome`, you would use the following command at the event procedure or module procedure that requires printing:

```
frmWelcome.PrintForm
```

If `frmWelcome` is the current form (its title bar is highlighted), you can leave off the form name as shown:

```
PrintForm
```

In addition, you can use the object name of `Me`, which refers to the current form and can be used in place of the form name as shown:

```
Me.PrintForm
```

THE `PrintForm` WEAKNESSES

The strength of `PrintForm` is in its simplicity. This method provides the most useful and simplest printer output within the Visual Basic environment. Unfortunately, with this simplicity comes a few problems you should know about.

- No matter how high of a resolution the printer supports, the `PrintForm` will print the form only at the screen's current resolution. Generally, this resolution goes no higher than 96 DPI (dots per inch). Usually printer resolutions are 300 DPI or higher. This results in a form that doesn't look as good on paper as it did on the screen.

- You must always make sure that the form's `AutoRedraw` property is set to `True` before you print any form that contains controls and other non-text graphic elements. By default, this property is `False`, meaning that the `Print` method prints directly on top of

any graphical controls on the form. If you set AutoRedraw to
True, the graphic image stays visible while PrintForm does its
thing behind the graphic and does not overwrite any of it. This
allows the form output to correctly appear on the printer.

CHECKING FOR PRINTER ERRORS

Any time you print, you should check for an error condition. The user's
printer might not be turned on, connected to the computer, or have paper
in it. Use the following On Error Goto command to notify the user of the
print problem:

```
Private Sub cmdPrintForm_Click ()
On Error GoTo ErrHandler
  frmAccPayable.PrintForm
  Exit Sub
ErrHandler:
  MsgBox("A printer problem exists", vbExclamation,
  ➥"Print Error")
End Sub
```

USING THE `Printers` COLLECTION

When Visual Basic prints data, it uses the Windows default printer.
Because Windows can have many different printers installed, Visual Basic
provides a way to access any of these printers using the Printers collection. To print information to a particular printer, you would first set that
printer as the default for Visual Basic. After you set the default printer,
Visual Basic will send any output from the program to that printer and
ignore the system's default printer until the application ends or you desig-
nate another printer in the application.

The Printers collection lists all the printers on the computer on which
the application is running. Therefore, the Printers collection list will be
different on every computer. A user could run your application once, add
or remove a printer, and then run the application again, and the Printers
collection list would be different.

> **Note** The Printers collection is actually the same list
> of printers that appears in the Name drop-down list
> box on the system's Print dialog box.

ACCESSING THE Printers COLLECTION

You reference the Printers collection using an index, where the first
printer (system default) has a value of 0, the second has a value of 1, and
so on. By using the Count property of the Printers collection, you can
determine how many printers are installed on the current computer. In
order to change or set the default printer for your application, you would
use the Set Printer statement as shown in the following example:

```
Set Printer = Printers(1)    'Change the default printer
```

THE PRINTER'S PROPERTIES

The printer's properties you will work with most often are listed in Table
16.1. Most of these properties have named constants associated with them
to allow you to test the properties against the named constants, such as
vbPRPSLetter, which are easier to understand than the actual numbers
they represent.

> **Tip** To see a list of the constants for a particular
> property, display that property in the online help ref-
> erence system.

TABLE 16.1 COMMON PRINTER OBJECT PROPERTIES

PROPERTY	DESCRIPTION
ColorMode	Determines whether the printer can print in color or black and white.
Copies	Specifies the number of copies the user wants.

continues

TABLE **16.1**   CONTINUED

PROPERTY	DESCRIPTION
CurrentX, CurrentY	Returns or sets the current X and Y coordinates where the next character (or drawing) will appear.
DeviceName	Contains the name of the printer, such as HP LaserJet 6P.
DriverName	Contains the name of the print driver. Many printers from the same company utilize the same printer driver supplied by the manufacturer.
Duplex	Determines whether the printer can print to both sides of the paper or to a single side.
Font	Returns certain font subproperty values that are set, such as Printer.Font.Bold.
FontCount	Returns the number of fonts supported by the printer.
Height	Returns the height of the printed page for the selected printer.
Orientation	Returns or sets the printer's portrait or landscape orientation.
Page	Returns the current page number.
PaperBin	Returns or sets the paper bin used for printing.
PaperSize	Returns or sets the paper size currently being used.
Port	Returns the name of the printer's port.
PrintQuality	Returns or sets the printer's resolution.

PROPERTY	DESCRIPTION
TrackDefault	When False, this property keeps the current printer property settings if you change default printers; when True, changes the printer property settings at runtime if you select a different default printer.
Width	Returns the width of the printed page for the selected printer.
Zoom	Returns or sets the percentage of scaling used for the printed output.

When your application starts, the printer properties for the Printer object match those of the Windows system default printer. If you select a new Visual Basic default printer, the properties change accordingly. At runtime, you can change many of these properties as described in Table 16.1.

The following code shows how to loop through the Printers collection looking for a particular printer and then setting it as the default when found:

```
Dim prnPrntr As Printer
For Each prnPrntr In Printers
   If prnPrntr.ColorMode = vbPRCMColor Then
     Set Printer = prnPrntr
     Exit For
   End If
Next
```

Notice the first line that declares a variable by the data type Printer. As you learn more about Visual Basic, you will notice that you can declare variables of virtually any data type, including Printer and Form. The Printer variable lets you access each printer on the system. An equivalent For statement would be

```
For prnPrntr = 1 to (Printers.Count - 1)
```

USING THE PRINT COMMON DIALOG

Many property settings that are accessible in the Printers collection require that you ask the user what settings or options he or she wants to use. By using the Common Dialog control's Print dialog box (see Figure 16.1), you can display the Windows Print dialog box that already lists the available printers on the computer. You would then take the information entered by the user from the form and change the properties of the default printer object.

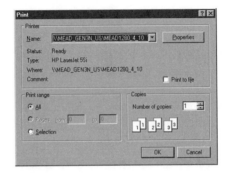

FIGURE 16.1   Using the Windows Common Dialog Print dialog box.

> **Note**   For more information on using the Windows CommonDialog control, see Lesson 15, "The Common Dialog Control."

PRINTING FROM VISUAL BASIC

Like everything else in Visual Basic, a specific object can be used to access the computer's default printer. The Printer object provides the reference to the default printer's property using the Printers collection discussed in the preceding section. Although programming with the Printer object can be tedious, you can and should create general-purpose output routines that will help you print information more easily within your application.

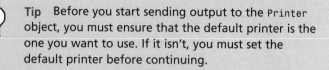

Tip Before you start sending output to the `Printer` object, you must ensure that the default printer is the one you want to use. If it isn't, you must set the default printer before continuing.

After you select a default printer, you use the `Printer` object to route text and graphics to that printer. In this section, you will learn how to create your output. In other words, you will send output to the `Printer` object. However, nothing will actually print until you execute a specific command in the program code. After you have completed the creation of your `Printer` object and are ready to send the completed output to the printer, you will use the `NewPage` or `EndDoc` methods to start the actual printing process.

Note If you don't use the `EndDoc` method in the code, printing can also start when the application ends.

PRINTING TO THE `Printer` OBJECT

One of the easiest ways to send output is to use the `Printer` object's `Print` method. The following example sends a message to the printer:

```
Printer.Print "This is a demo of printing to the
➥default printer"
```

To begin the printing at the top of a page or to go to a new page at any time, use the `NewPage` method as shown in the following code:

```
Printer.NewPage
```

SETTING PAGE MARGINS

When printing, you might want to create margins on the page that the subsequent `Printer` methods will use. Table 16.2 lists the properties that you would use to set the margins for the printer.

TABLE 16.2   MARGIN PROPERTIES

PROPERTY	DESCRIPTION
ScaleLeft	Defines the printable area's extreme left X page coordinate.
ScaleMode	Determines the measurement value used for scaling. Generally, a ScaleMode of VbPoints (the value of 2), vbCharacters (the printer's default character width), VbInches, or VbCentimeters are used for text printing.
ScaleHeight	Changes the Printer object's vertical coordinate system.
ScaleTop	Defines the printable area's extreme top Y page coordinate.
ScaleWidth	Changes the Printer object's horizontal coordinate system.

To set the top margin to six characters and the left margin to ten characters, you can use the following statements:

```
Printer.ScaleMode = vbCharacters
Printer.ScaleTop = 6
Printer.ScaleLeft = 10
```

Any Printer methods that follow these statements would use these boundaries.

CANCELING AN OUTPUT

Visual Basic's Printer object supports several methods that let you control the printing process. As you have seen, you can move the printing to the top of a page using the NewPage method and start the print process using the EndDoc method. At any point during the preparation of the output, but before the EndDoc method is issued, you can cancel the output by issuing the KillDoc method as shown:

```
Printer.KillDoc
```

KillDoc completely removes your output from the Printer object. If you decide later that you really wanted to print the information, you would have to re-execute the section of code that built the output the first time.

 Caution KillDoc cannot cancel a print job that has already started to print. In addition, KillDoc will not terminate a PrintForm job.

SUMMARY

This lesson covered the Printers collection and its associated Printer object, which enables you to interact with the printers that are installed on the computer. By using the properties of the Printer object, you can set the default printer and modify the different settings for the printer. In addition, you learned how to print an entire form with only one line of program code.

LESSON 17

DEALING WITH BUGS

This lesson identifies different types of problems you might encounter and how to use the tools that assist you in that process.

Designing and coding your application is only the first part of the process that you perform when creating a professional application. After you have finished coding the application, you must test it to make sure it works correctly, and then fix any problems that you might find. This chapter briefly discusses the different types of problems you must watch out for. In addition, you learn how to use the tools included with Visual Basic that assist you in the process.

THINK FIRST, CODE LATER

The best way to find and fix problems is to prevent them from happening. The way to do this is to spend the time to think through what you want the application to do and create a design or plan to work from. Most programmers do not spend enough time analyzing and designing the applications that they build. They would much rather jump right in and start coding. However, having a good design will keep you from having to guess what to do next. Paying attention to that design will help you minimize the number of often problematic changes to an application.

After you have a good design to work with, you can start coding your application. This is where the fun begins. In Visual Basic, the testing cycle of an application is shortened because Visual Basic will stop the application whenever it encounters a bug or problem it doesn't know how to handle. It is important to remember that a single bug might cause other problems later in the application process. So, if you fix the one root bug, you will have removed tons of other bugs you might not have been aware of.

DEFINING THE PROBLEM

Problems come in many different forms within an application. They can range from the annoying (misspelled variables) to the serious (Windows terminates) to the deadly (lost data). To the user of the application, a problem or bug is anything that doesn't match the expected results. However, to a programmer, a bug is something that produces unexpected results or prevents the application from executing. When you start testing the application, you should have a plan to follow that will prevent you from jumping all over the application as you test. By testing in a logical pattern, you can be confident that you will find almost all the bugs.

FINDING THE PROBLEM

Finding where a bug happened in an application is not an easy process. Because Visual Basic stops the application when a problem occurs, it enables you to at least identify the section of code to look in. In fact, Visual Basic will usually display an error message telling you what type of error has occurred (see Figure 17.1). Although Visual Basic will tell you where the error is, it does not fix it for you or tell you how to fix it.

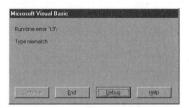

FIGURE 17.1   A typical error message from Visual Basic.

Even more confusing is that the actual problem might have occurred much earlier in the application. This means that you will have to execute the application a single line of code at a time to find the actual problem. Thankfully, Visual Basic provides several tools that enable you to look at how the application is executed. In addition, they enable you to observe or watch how variables and property settings change during the execution of the application. What you are really doing during this process is lifting the hood off the application and checking out how the engine works.

Unfortunately, there are no instant fixes for bugs and problems in an application. Finding and fixing them takes time and hard work. Basically, debugging helps you to understand what is going on during the execution of the application. The better you understand how the application works, the faster you can find the bugs.

WHEN ERRORS CROP UP

When errors occur, you must first identify what is causing the error and then fix it. Visual Basic provides several very good tools for testing and debugging your application, including a method for stopping your application at a particular line of code or when the contents of a variable or property change in the code. In addition, you can modify the code during the test and change the contents of a variable or property.

The Visual Basic environment works in three different processing modes as you code and test your application. When you are in the process of writing the code for the application, you are in Visual Basic's Design mode. When you are running the application, you are in Run mode, and when you are debugging the application, you will be working in Break mode. Knowing which mode you are in is easy; just look at the Visual Basic title bar. The title bar always displays the current mode, as shown in Figure 17.2.

The current mode is displayed

FIGURE 17.2   Identifying the current working mode.

STOPPING THE PROGRAM

In Design mode, you can modify the design or code of the application but you cannot see how the changes will impact the application process. In Run mode, you can watch the application process but cannot modify the design or code. By using Break mode, you can stop the application and look at the variables and objects at that moment. The contents of variables and properties are retained, so you can analyze the current state of the application. While in Break mode you can perform the following actions:

- Modify program code.

- View changes to the form interface.

- Display a list of called procedures.

- View the values of variables, properties, and statements.

- Change the values of variables and properties.

- Set the next statement to execute.

- Execute program statements using the Immediate window.

During the testing process, you will probably want to stop the application at certain sections of code. By setting a breakpoint, you can do just that. To see how this works, open the Calc project that can be found in the Visual Basic samples directory. Then, display the code for the Number_Click routine (see Figure 17.3).

```
Calc - Calculator [Code]                                    _ □ ×
Number                      ▼    Click                          ▼
    ' Click event procedure for number keys (0-9).
    ' Append new number to the number in the display.
    Private Sub Number_Click(Index As Integer)
        If LastInput <> "NUMS" Then
            Readout = Format(0, ".")
            DecimalFlag = False
        End If
        If DecimalFlag Then
            Readout = Readout + Number(Index).Caption
        Else
            Readout = Left(Readout, InStr(Readout, Format(0, ".")))
        End If
        If LastInput = "NEG" Then Readout = "-" & Readout
        LastInput = "NUMS"
    End Sub
```

FIGURE 17.3   Displaying the code to test.

To set a breakpoint, simply click in the margin area to the left of the program line where you want to stop. This will change the background color of that line and place a dot in the margin, as shown in Figure 17.4.

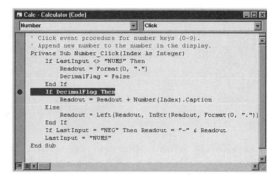

FIGURE 17.4   Setting a breakpoint.

Now, execute the application and click a number on the form. This will stop the application at the specified line of code, highlighting it in a different color (see Figure 17.5).

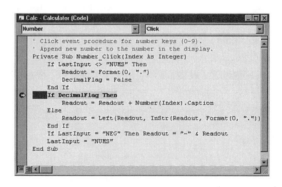

FIGURE 17.5   Execution of the application stops at the breakpoint.

Visual Basic actually stops the execution of the program just before the line containing the breakpoint. If you want to see what happens when that line is executed, you can single step the application by pressing the F8 key on the keyboard. This will execute the current statement and stop.

If you want to display the value of a variable, you can rest the mouse on the variable; Visual Basic will display the value of the variable in a ToolTip box (see Figure 17.6).

FIGURE **17.6**   Displaying variable values using the pop-up ToolTips.

USING THE IMMEDIATE WINDOW

You can use the Immediate window whenever the program has been paused either at a breakpoint or when single stepping. It enables you to change the values of the variables in your program, giving you the chance to test for conditions that are very hard to produce normally. In addition, you can also display the contents of a variable or property, as shown in Figure 17.7.

```
Immediate
?Number(Index).Caption
5
```

FIGURE **17.7**   You use the Immediate window to execute a single line of Visual Basic code.

If you want to change the value of a variable or property to see how it will affect the application process, you can execute an assignment statement in the Immediate window, as shown in Figure 17.8.

```
Immediate
Decimal_Flag = -1
?decimal_flag
-1
|
```

FIGURE **17.8**   Modifying the values of the variable.

WATCHING VARIABLES

During the debugging process, you might find that a calculation or function is not producing the results that you want, or problems might be occurring when a particular variable or property contains a certain value. The Watch expression tools enable you to monitor these variables and expressions in your application. They can be specified when in Design or Debug mode and will be displayed when in Debug mode in the Watches dialog box. The Add Watch dialog box prompts you for the information needed to set the Watch expression (see Figure 17.9).

FIGURE 17.9   Using the Add Watch dialog box to set a Watch expression for testing.

The easiest way to set a Watch expression is to select the variable or expression you want to watch and then choose **Add Watch** from the **Debug** menu. This will place the correct information into the Add Watch dialog box. The only thing you would need to select is the type of watch you want by clicking one of the three option buttons at the bottom of the form. The default setting, **Watch Expression**, will display the value of the expression but will not stop the execution of the program if it changes. After you start the debugging session, the Watches window will display all the different watches for you to view using a unique icon for each type of Watch expression (see Figure 17.10).

Break when true

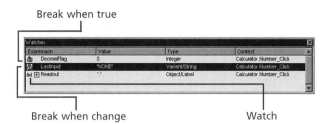

Break when change   Watch

FIGURE **17.10**   Displaying values in the Watches window.

SUMMARY

Learning how to debug an application is a very personal and unique process. No one person can really teach someone else how to debug a program. The most that can be done is to show you how to use the tools available and explain the process. You will develop your own techniques for debugging as you go. Hopefully, this chapter has given you some ideas on how to determine the problems in your application and, by using the tools, locate and fix them.

LESSON 18

USING THE DATA FORM WIZARD

In this lesson, you will learn how to use the Data Form Wizard, which is one of the many wizards that come with Visual Basic. In particular, this wizard assists you in creating fully functional data access forms that you can then add to your application.

CREATING A DATA FORM

In Lesson 14, "Connecting to the Database," you learned what it takes to connect to a database and then manually create a form that contains bound controls that display data from the database. Now that you know how tedious and difficult this can be, you will see how to use the supplied Data Form Wizard to perform most of the process for you. By providing the Data Form Wizard, Visual Basic has made it very easy to create and include data-bound forms that give the user complete access to the data in the application's database. The Data Form Wizard automatically generates forms that contain individual bound controls and procedures used to manage the data obtained from the database. The Data Form Wizard can be used to create single-query forms to access data from a single table or query, master/detail-type forms to manage more complex, one-to-many data relationships, or grid forms to manage data all at once.

The wizard steps through several dialog boxes and prompts you for the information needed to build the data form properly. However, because the form that the wizard will create is fairly generic, you will probably want to modify it later to resemble the rest of the forms in your application. To see how this wizard works, start a new project, and open the **Data Form Wizard** from the **Add-Ins** menu.

> **Note** If the Data Form Wizard is not on the **Add-Ins** menu, you must add it by using the Add-Ins Manager.

The first dialog box displayed is the Introduction dialog box. If you have previously used this wizard, you could select a data form profile that you previously saved. Click **Next** to choose the database type you are working with. At this time, there are only two database types to choose from: Microsoft Access and open database connectivity (ODBC). Choose **Access** and click **Next** to continue. After you've selected your database type, you must specify the actual database location or your connection information. For Access, you are prompted for the database location as shown in Figure 18.1. However, if you are using ODBC, you will be prompted for the appropriate connection information as shown in Figure 18.2.

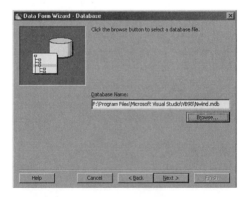

FIGURE **18.1**   Specifying the Access database.

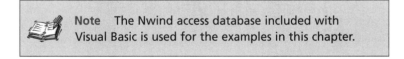

> **Note** The Nwind access database included with Visual Basic is used for the examples in this chapter.

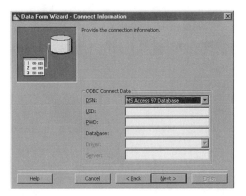

FIGURE 18.2   Setting the ODBC connection information.

Locate and select the **NorthWind database (NWIND.MDB)** on your computer, select it, and then click **Next** to continue. As you move to the next dialog box, the wizard actually connects to and opens the specified database. The Form dialog box in Figure 18.3 asks you to enter a name for the new form, the form layout you want to create, and the type of data access connection to use.

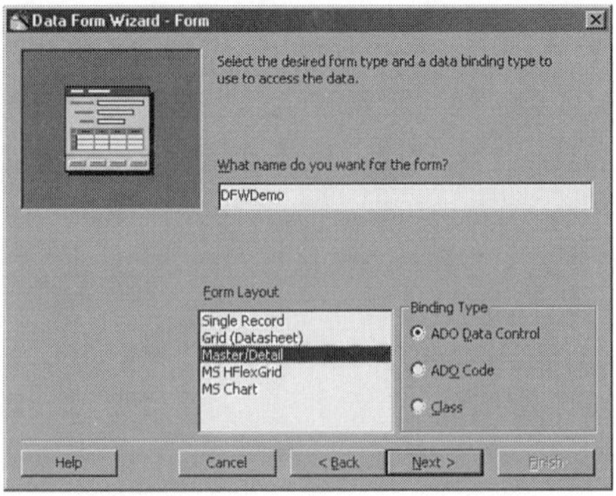

FIGURE 18.3   Selecting the form layout and data access.

Because each form layout requires different information, the remaining steps will vary depending on the layout you've selected. For this example, choose the **Master/Detail** form layout and leave the default **Binding Type** of **ADO Data Control.** Finally, name the form DFWDemo and click the **Next** button. Because you selected the Master/Detail layout, you will be prompted for the record source and fields for both the master and the detail queries. The first dialog box, Master Record Source, requests the master query source (see Figure 18.4).

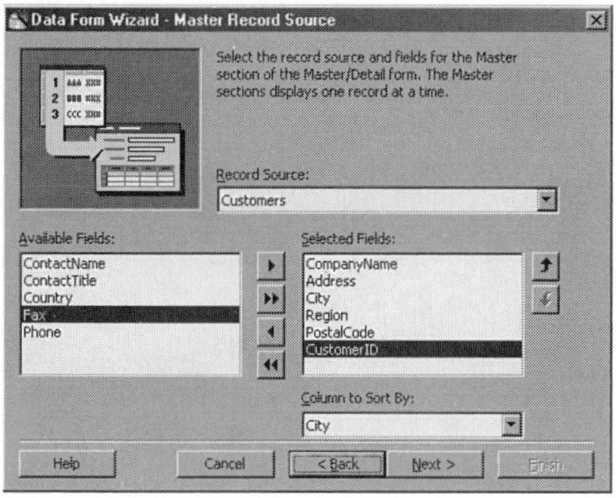

FIGURE 18.4   Setting the Master Record Source.

From the **Record Source** drop-down, select the **Customers** table, and then select the fields shown in Figure 18.4. Finally, set the sort column to **City** and click the **Next** button to define the detail query information. As you can see from Figure 18.5, the Detail Record Source dialog box looks exactly like the Master dialog box.

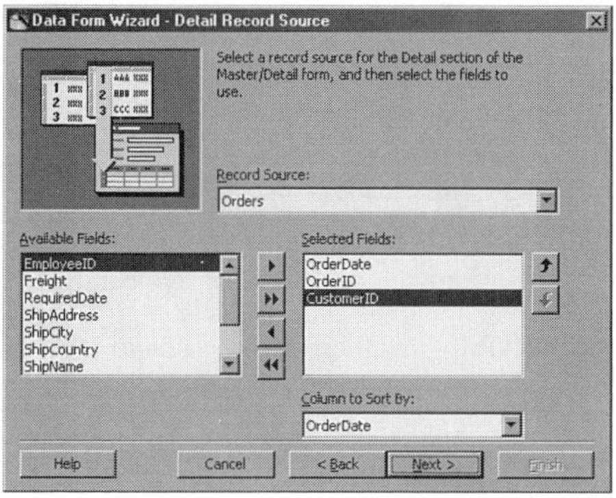

FIGURE 18.5   Setting the Detail Record Source.

Select the **Orders** table from the **Record Source** drop-down, and then select the fields shown in Figure 18.5. Set the sort column to **OrderDate** and click **Next** to continue. The Record Source Relation dialog box prompts you to set the relationship or the "join" between the Master and Detail queries (see Figure 18.6).

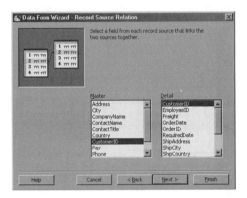

FIGURE **18.6**   Defining the relationship between the two record source queries.

For the selected tables, the CustomerID should be used to link the two sources. After setting this link, click **Next** to continue. The Control Selection dialog box lets you choose from the available data navigation and manipulation controls you might want on the form, and then tells the wizard to create the associated code for each selected control (see Figure 18.7). You can choose from the following available controls:

- **Add Button**—Places an **Add** button on the form with the associated code to add new records to the database.

- **Update Button**—Adds the **Update** button and its associated code to update the database from the form. This button is available only if you are using the Data Control Binding type.

- **Delete Button**—Provides the ability to delete records from the database.

- **Refresh Button**—Adds the code and command button to allow the user to request a database refresh.

- **Close Button**—Includes the code and the command button to close the data form.

- **Show Data Control**—If this check box is clicked, the data control will be displayed on the form.

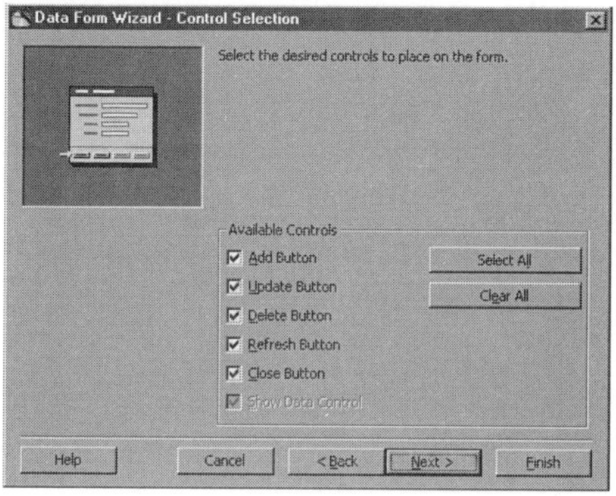

FIGURE **18.7**   Selecting the Data Command buttons.

Leaving the defaults, click **Next** to save these settings to use later and then finish the process by clicking the **Finish** button. The Data Form Wizard will now perform its magic and create the form shown in Figure 18.8.

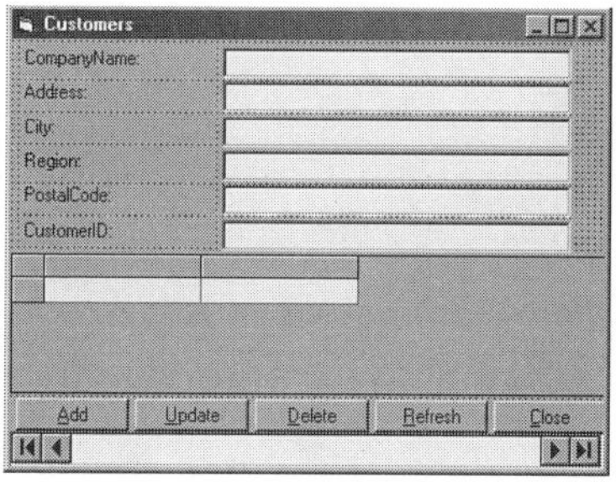

FIGURE **18.8**   The finished data form created by the wizard.

To see how this actually works, add a command button to the default form with the following code in its Click event routine:

```
DFWDemo.Show
```

This statement will display the new data form you created when the command button is clicked. Now, run the application, and click the command button to display the data form. You should see one customer at a time with all the customer's orders listed in the grid, as shown in Figure 18.9.

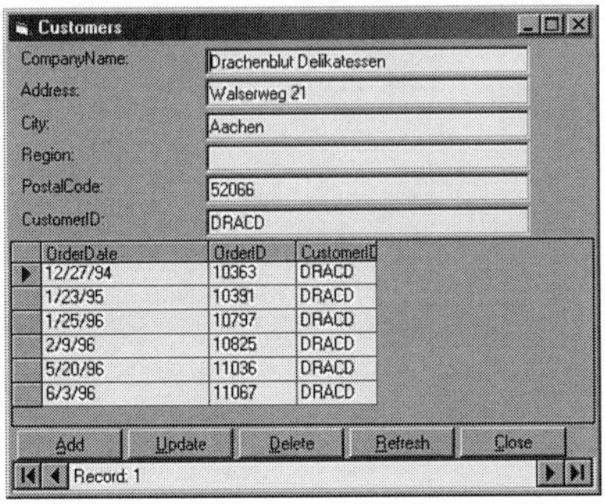

FIGURE **18.9** The finished data form created by the wizard.

Using the data control at the bottom of the form, you can move from one customer to another, while at the same time you will see the order information change. By using the Data Form Wizard, you can create data-aware applications with very little effort. However, the wizard only creates the forms with the initial program code that might be required. You must maintain the form's layout and its associated code after the form is created.

SUMMARY

This lesson showed you how to use the Data Form Wizard included with Visual Basic. By using this wizard, you can reduce the amount of work and time required to create the initial data-bound forms you will need for a database application. In Lesson 19, "Using the Application Wizard," you are going to see how to use the Application Wizard that will actually create a working application shell for you to modify.

LESSON 19

USING THE APPLICATION WIZARD

In this lesson, you learn how to use the Application Wizard that comes with Visual Basic.

INTRODUCING THE APPLICATION WIZARD

Now that you have been through most of this book, you have probably figured out that many of the initial tasks required to create a new project are the same no matter what type of application you want to create. The Application Wizard brings together all the tasks, skills, and components you have learned in this book, and many others you haven't seen, to build what is called an application prototype. A *prototype* is a working application without the code that turns it into a specific application. In English, this means you can

- Run the application
- Click menu options
- Click toolbar options
- Navigate from form to form

However, other than displaying forms, there is no actual application-specific processing in the prototype. You must add the code and controls required on the forms. The wizard only automates the common starting tasks.

USING THE WIZARD

When you are ready to start a new application project, you must decide whether to use the Application Wizard to create the basic forms or create them from scratch. If you're like me, you'll use the Application Wizard. So start Visual Basic, if it's not already started, and then choose **Application Wizard** from the dialog box that appears when you launch Visual Basic.

When the wizard starts, you will see the Introduction dialog box, which explains that the wizard is about to start. If you have previously used the Visual Basic Application Wizard and saved the settings in a profile, you might want to select that profile's settings for this application. If this is not the case, leave the **Extra Profile** setting at **None**, and click the **Next** button to continue.

The following wizard screen prompts you to select an interface type. The following are the available options:

- **Multiple Document Interface (MDI)**—This option enables your application to contain multiple document windows in a parent/child window configuration. Microsoft Word is a good example of an MDI application in which each document you have open is a child of the parent Microsoft Word window.

- **Single Document Interface (SDI)**—This option allows your application to have open only one document window at a time. Notepad is an example of an SDI application.

- **Explorer Style**—This option allows your application to have a Windows Explorer-type interface. This is also known as a tree view, with index or summary information in the left pane and detailed information in the right pane.

In Figure 19.1, notice that the upper-left window displays a sample program for each interface type as you make your selection. Select the **Single Document Interface** option, and name your project MyProject (no spaces allowed) before clicking **Next** to continue.

The Menus window, shown in Figure 19.2, offers you the option to select standard menu and submenu selections for your application. After you have set the menu items to what you need in your applications, click **Next** to proceed.

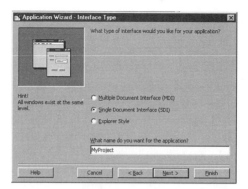

FIGURE 19.1   Select the interface type for your application.

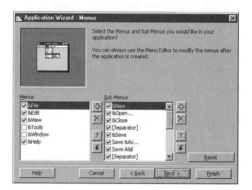

FIGURE 19.2   Select the options you want your application's menu to contain.

> **Tip**   You might notice that some menu options aren't in the order in which you'd expect to see them. Each interface will change how the menu options are displayed. If you want to change the order, go right ahead. If you think you'll forget an option, you can always add it later. For now, the default menu options are fine.

The Customize Toolbar wizard screen, shown in Figure 19.3, offers a default set of buttons for the style you selected and the option of modifying those toolbar buttons for your application. The list on the left displays the available toolbar buttons, and the list on the right lists the buttons and separator spaces on your application's toolbar. The current image of your application's toolbar is displayed near the top of the window. You can change the order of the buttons by using the up and down arrows. You may also add external images with the Image Control button. Again, when you are satisfied with your toolbar selections, click **Next** to continue.

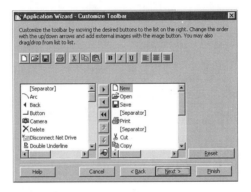

FIGURE 19.3   Creating a toolbar for your application.

Don't worry if you forget a menu item or toolbar button, you can always add them manually later.

The Resources screen, shown in Figure 19.4, offers the opportunity to use resource files to store the strings used in your application. These resource files, which would then house the strings for the various prompts and dialog boxes in your application, are then added to your application. If you aren't sure if you want to use a resource file, there's really no harm in choosing **Yes** on this dialog box. If you do choose to use a resource file, you must enter a path and filename. Either way, click **Next** to continue.

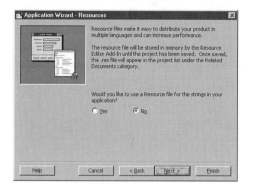

Note If you choose to use the resource file option, the menu captions will look a little strange at design time. Because the actual captions are in the resource file, they're displayed only at runtime.

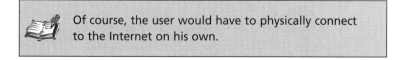

FIGURE 19.4   Resource file selection.

The next wizard screen, shown in Figure 19.5, is the Internet Connectivity screen. From this screen, you can add an Internet browser interface to your application. If you select **Yes** from this window (please *don't* select **Yes** here), the Application Wizard will add a complete Internet browser to your application that would operate much like Internet Explorer. Without any programming on your part, your application's user will be able to access the Internet. By providing a valid Internet address, such as http://www.*mywebsite*.com, the application's browser window will display that Web page in the application's browser window.

Of course, the user would have to physically connect to the Internet on his own.

FIGURE 19.5   Internet Connectivity settings.

The Standard Forms screen, shown in Figure 19.6, enables you to add any of the following available standard forms to your application:

- **Splash screen at application start up**—This is a title screen that displays when your program first executes.

- **Login dialog to accept an ID and Password**—This is a dialog box that prompts for a user's ID and password.

- **Options dialog for custom settings**—This is a tabbed blank dialog box for the user to specify settings for your application.

- **About Box**—This is an example of a dialog box that appears when your users select **Help, About** from your application's menu.

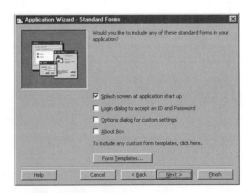

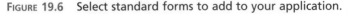

FIGURE 19.6   Select standard forms to add to your application.

You could also select the **Form Templates** button and select from any of the form templates included with Visual Basic or any form templates that you've created, as shown in Figure 19.7.

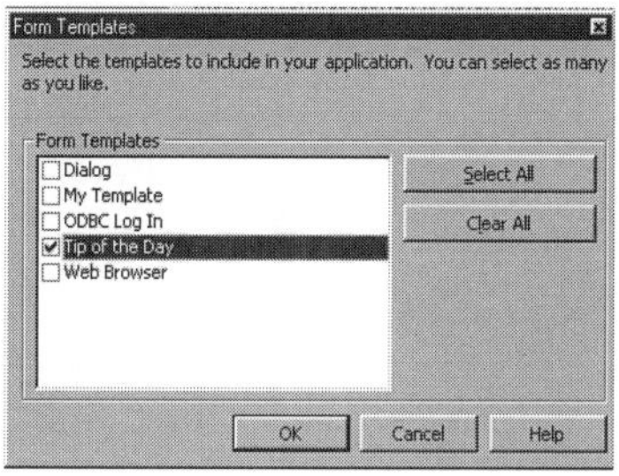

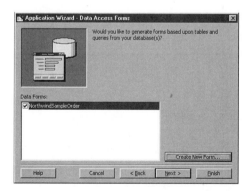

FIGURE **19.7**   Selecting from the form templates.

As shown in Figure 19.8, you can next add a data form to your application. You can either select an existing data form or click the **Create New Form** button to launch the Data Form Wizard (see chapter 18, "Using the Data Form Wizard") to create one now.

FIGURE **19.8**   Selecting a data form to add to your application.

> Although the Data Form Wizard is available at any time, if you add the data forms now, the Application Wizard will add the menu items and code to display these forms in the application.

The Visual Basic Data Form Wizard enables you to create a form based on data records. Click **Next** to complete the process.

You have now provided the Application Wizard with all the information it needs to create your application prototype. If you want to save the settings you've just selected as a template to use for other applications, click the ellipsis (...) to select a profile file to save your settings for future use. When you use a saved profile later, you can always change any settings required for that project.

When you click **Finish**, the wizard will create your application's shell. After completing the process, the Visual Basic Application Wizard displays a dialog box letting you know that your application has been created. When you click **OK**, you are in the development environment with your application's shell loaded (see Figure 19.9). At this point, your application can run (depending on the options you have selected), but there is no code to tell the application exactly what functions to perform.

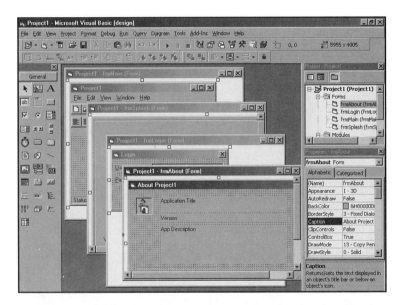

FIGURE 19.9   The final application prototype project in Visual Basic.

When you click the **View Report** button, the Visual Basic Application Wizard displays a report that you can view or save as a text file. This report provides instructions for filling in your application's shell and completing the application.

Your prototype is now ready for you to start adding the code it needs to perform the specific tasks required.

SUMMARY

This lesson covered how to create an application using the Visual Basic Application Wizard. As you have seen, this is a lot easier than creating it by hand. Of course, there is still work that needs to be done before this prototype is a real application that can be used.

LESSON 20

CREATING THE APPLICATION'S EXE FILE

This lesson discusses the packaging and deployment of your application, as well as the creation of the executable program file.

When you first start creating applications with Visual Basic, you will probably spend a large amount of time and effort designing, creating, and testing your application. You have also spent some time learning Visual Basic itself, so that you can create the application. If you have made it through the process, you have created a working application. But, what do you do with it? How do you distribute it to others?

At the moment, your application will only execute within the Visual Basic development environment. You cannot expect everyone who wants to use your application to go out and purchase Visual Basic. So, you must create an executable copy of your application that doesn't require the development environment. This chapter discusses several important topics that deal with the packaging and deployment of your application, including the creation of the executable (or .EXE) program file.

WHAT MAKES UP AN APPLICATION?

Distributing your application takes a lot more than putting the files on disks and selling or giving it to others. The complete application package consists of many different elements. Some of these topics require a design effort almost as long as the application itself. Most of the issues that go into making a professional application package fall into one of the following categories:

- Program design
- Reporting

- Performance

- Error handling

- Documentation

- Physical packaging

- Customer support

As you can see from this list, many areas have nothing to do with programming. The best way to know what you should do for these topics is to investigate other Windows products and start a list of the things you like and dislike about the way they do things. This will give you a starting point for your own application.

COMPILING THE APPLICATION

Now that you are at the point of distributing the application, you should first create the executable version of it to make sure it works outside the Visual Basic development environment. Compiling your application into an executable is really quite simple. There are, however, a few properties that you should set before actually making an EXE file. The Properties page of the project can be displayed by pulling down the **Project** menu and choosing *<Project>* **Properties**. The dialog box in Figure 20.1 appears.

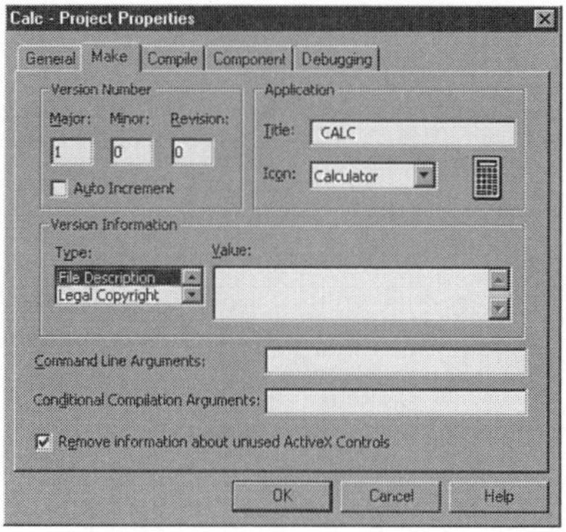

FIGURE 20.1   Setting the properties of the project that are used during the compile process.

There are many tabs on this Properties page, but the **Make** tab enables
you to set what information will be saved with the project when it is compiled. Windows uses this information to display the properties of the executable file (see Figure 20.2). The information will also be used by the
Packaging and Deployment Wizard, which is discussed in the next
section.

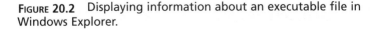

FIGURE 20.2   Displaying information about an executable file in
Windows Explorer.

To actually compile the project, pull down the **File** menu and choose
Make *Project*.EXE, where ***Project*** is the name of the project you are
working with. This will display a Make *Project* dialog box, in which you
can specify the location for Visual Basic to write the executable file to.
Finally, click the **OK** button to create the EXE file. This will complete the
process. You should now find the *Project*.exe file in that directory and
execute it to make sure it runs properly. If it doesn't, you must investigate
what the problem is before creating the distribution package.

DISTRIBUTING THE APPLICATION

After you have completed your application and are satisfied that you have
tested it enough, you are ready to distribute it. Before there was Windows,
you could fit most applications on one disk, making it very easy to distribute to users. You only needed to copy the files onto the disk, and then
when someone wanted to use it, he simply copied it onto his computer.

Unfortunately, it is not that easy any more. These days, the Windows environment requires you to register support files, and Visual Basic needs many files to be installed with your application for it to run properly. This makes merely copying files onto a computer a thing of the past. More support files are required by your application than you might realize. Even a small Visual Basic application requires many files that provide the access to the controls and database commands that your application is using. In addition, there are many more ways to distribute the application than just on disk, including the following:

- Disks

- CD-ROM

- Network installation

- Internet installation

Each method requires slightly different installation files and setup. The following are the two main steps that you will perform for your application:

- Packaging—You must create a set of cabinet (.CAB) files that contain all the files your application requires.

- Deployment—The packaged application must be copied to the distribution media you will be using.

> **Note**   A .CAB file is a compressed file that is designed for the distribution of a large number of files in the smallest amount of space.

As with almost anything else in Visual Basic, a wizard is included to assist you in the packaging and deployment of your application. The Packaging and Deployment Wizard actually replaces the older Application Setup Wizard that had been a part of Visual Basic since version 1. The new wizard automates much of the work involved in creating and deploying these files. The wizard offers three options for you to use:

- Package—Assists you in packaging the project's files into cabinet files that can then be deployed, and in most cases the setup program that will be used to install the application.

- Deploy—Sets up and copies the packaged application to the appropriate distribution media.

- Manage Scripts—Provides maintenance for the scripts that have been saved from previous packaging and deployment sessions.

CREATING THE PACKAGE

The Packaging and Deployment Wizard helps you create a complete installation system for your application. In addition to creating a standard installation, it also includes the files and programs needed to allow users to remove or uninstall the application from their computers. The application package consists of the .CAB file or files that contain the compressed project files and any other support files the user will need to install and use your application. The wizard can create two distinct types of packages, one for distributing on disk or CD-ROM and the other for distributing the application across the Internet. No matter which package you are creating, there is a single set of steps you must perform to create the package.

1. Select the package type.
2. Specify the files to distribute.
3. Choose the location for the installation.
4. Create the package.
5. Deploy the package.

When using the wizard, you will step through the process and be prompted for the information required to build the package. The final step in the process is actually compressing the files into the cabinet files and then copying them to the specified location. If you have chosen to create a disk installation, you will be asked to supply the disks to which to copy the files.

USING THE PACKAGING AND DEPLOYMENT WIZARD

Start the wizard by selecting it from the Windows **Start** menu, as shown in Figure 20.3.

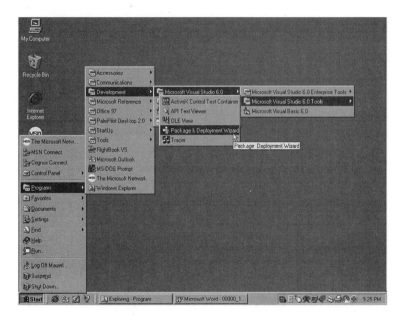

FIGURE 20.3   Starting the Packaging and Deployment Wizard.

In the first dialog box you will see, you must enter the name and location of the Visual Basic project you want to package. It also presents the three main options for you to choose from (see Figure 20.4).

After you have selected the project, click the **Package** button to start the creation process. You will see that the wizard is analyzing the project before displaying the next dialog box, which asks you the package type to create. Only two items are listed—the first will create an installation package for the application. The second option will create a file that contains the list of the required files for the application to be installed properly. Choose the first option, and click **Next**. If the wizard cannot find the compiled executable, a message will be displayed asking you to browse for the executable or compile the project.

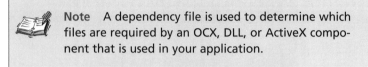

> **Note** A dependency file is used to determine which files are required by an OCX, DLL, or ActiveX component that is used in your application.

FIGURE 20.4   Specifying the project to package and choosing the processing option.

This dialog box (see Figure 20.5) asks you to select the location in which you want the package files to be written to. Select the path you want to use, and click **Next** to continue. If the path you specify does not exist, you will be asked if you want to create it.

FIGURE 20.5   Specifying the location in which to build the application package.

The next dialog box displays the list of files that the wizard has determined are needed for your application. In addition, if your application requires some files that are not listed, click the **Add** button to add them now. Some of the files that you might have to add are

- Help files

- Database files

- Any documentation files

- ReadMe text files

When you are satisfied that the list is complete, click the **Next** button to specify the cabinet options to use when packaging the files. You can select either a single cabinet (which is usually used for CD or Internet installations) or multiple cabinets (used for disk installations). If you choose the **Multiple** cabinet option, you must specify the size of the disk you are using. After selecting the cabinet option, click **Next** to specify the title that will be seen on the Installation screen. After entering the title for your application, click **Next** to continue. The next dialog box (see Figure 20.6) allows you to define the **Start** menu group name and items that will be included in the group, as well as the icons to be used.

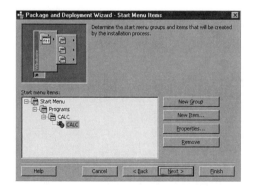

FIGURE 20.6   The wizard enables you to define exactly what the Start menu will contain and what icons are used.

The only item placed in the group by the wizard is the application itself. You might want to add an item for the following:

- Help system

- ReadMe file

- Any utility program that is included with the application

After you have finished setting up the start group, click **Next** to continue. The next two dialog boxes enable you to check and possibly modify the locations in which the files will be installed on the user's computer, and whether any of the application files are to be installed as shared files. You can accept the defaults at this time by clicking the **Next** button twice.

You are now prompted to name and save the packaging script that is created for you to use at a later time. At this point you have finished the process. Click the **Finish** button to actually create the package. After the packaging process is completed, you will once again be at the main wizard menu.

DEPLOYING THE PACKAGE

Now that you have a complete installation package for your application, you must create the deployment set for it. The Deployment option of the wizard can be used to actually deploy the application to disk, CD, or the Internet. Deploying your application requires the following steps:

1. Select the package to deploy.

2. Choose the deployment method.

3. Specify the deployment location.

From the main wizard dialog box, select the project for which you just created the package, and click the **Deploy** button. This displays a dialog box that asks you to select the packaging script you have just saved. This enables you to support different types of deployment by repeating the packaging process for each of the different deployment types and then saving the scripts. Choose the package you created, and click **Next**. You are now prompted for the type of deployment you want to perform. The two available deployment types are

- Folder

- Web publishing

Choose the **Folder** option and click **Next**. This dialog box asks you to select the location in which you want the finished deployment files to be written to (see Figure 20.7).

FIGURE 20.7   Deploying the package to a specific location on a hard drive or floppy disk drive.

After specifying the location, click **Next** to enter the name of the deployment script, and then click **Finish** to complete the process.

MANAGING SCRIPTS

The third function of the wizard provides the capability to duplicate, rename, or delete a packaging or deployment script when you no longer need it (see Figure 20.8).

FIGURE 20.8   Managing the scripts using the Packaging and Deployment Wizard.

If you must make a change to a script, you should use this option to make a copy of the original before continuing.

 Caution   If you delete a packaging script, the deployment function will not recognize the package that was created from that script as one that it can deploy.

TESTING THE INSTALLATION PACKAGE

Now that you have finished the packaging and deployment process, the last step is to test the installation process on another computer. You must do this to ensure that every file needed by your application is included in the installation cabinet files. If you test the installation process on a computer that has Visual Basic already installed on it, you will never really know whether the installation works. All the required Visual Basic files are already loaded on that computer.

SUMMARY

In this lesson, you learned the issues involved in distributing your application. There are many different things that you must be concerned with besides the application program itself. These issues should be dealt with as the application is being developed. Then when you are ready to distribute it, you can use the Packaging and Deployment Wizard to create the installation package and the required files so that users can install your application on their computers.

LESSON 21

SUPPORT AND MORE INFORMATION

This lesson discusses the different methods available to you to answer questions, get help, and fix problems in Visual Basic.

Besides learning how to use Visual Basic to design and create Windows applications, you also must understand how to get the information you will need to assist you in the process. This means being able to get the answers to questions ranging from a simple syntax question to a more detailed question on how to use a feature or control.

In addition, you must know where you can find the answers you need when there are problems with the Visual Basic environment or with the language itself. Visual Basic comes with several features that help you with these issues, and if you still need help, Microsoft provides a Web site that gives you more information, including any upgrades that might be available for Visual Basic.

AUTOMATIC CODE COMPLETION

The features you will use the most are built right into the Visual Basic Code Editor and can be used immediately. These include the following:

- Auto List Members
- Auto Quick Info

When entering code into the Code Editor, you will sometimes need to know the syntax of a command statement or the available methods and properties of an object. Visual Basic makes it easier for you to enter code by automatically filling in statements, properties, and arguments. As you enter code, the editor displays lists of appropriate choices, methods, or properties. To enable or disable any of these options, select **Tools, Options**, and then select the **Editor** tab, as shown in Figure 21.1.

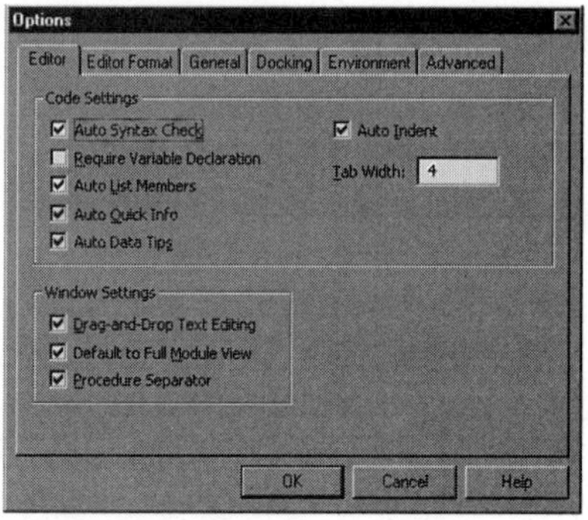

FIGURE 21.1   Setting the automatic code completion properties for the Visual Basic environment.

AUTO LIST MEMBERS

When you enter the name of a control or object in your code, this feature presents a drop-down list of properties and methods available for that control or object (see Figure 21.2). When you type the first few letters of the property or method name, the name is selected in the list. If you press the Tab key, the editor will complete the typing for you. This option is very useful if you do not remember all the available properties or methods for the object you are working with.

FIGURE 21.2   Choosing a property or method from the list members drop-down list.

> **Tip** If you do not want to use this feature, you can still display the list of available properties and methods by pressing the Ctrl+J key combination.

AUTO QUICK INFO

As you enter a Visual Basic statement or function, the Auto Quick Info feature displays the syntax of a statement or function for you (see Figure 21.3). When you enter the name of any valid statement or function, the syntax is shown with the first argument in bold.

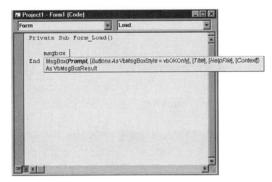

FIGURE **21.3**   Using the Auto Quick Info feature to assist in the coding of statements and functions.

As you enter the arguments for the statement or function that you are coding, the arguments of that statement will be bolded in turn, showing you which argument you are at within the statement.

> **Tip** If you do not want to use this feature, you can still display the syntax of the statement or function by pressing the Ctrl+I key combination.

USING MSDN HELP

The Visual Basic Help environment has been redone using the new HTML Help design and display. Included with this change is the installation of the Microsoft Developer Network (MSDN) Library with Visual Basic. The MSDN Library contains more than a gigabyte of developer information, documentation, sample code, technical articles, and more. You can access the MSDN Library on your computer in several ways. If you are in the Visual Basic environment, you can do the following:

- Display the MSDN Help by selecting an object or command and pressing the F1 key to display help for that specific topic.

- Display the MSDN Library by choosing **Help Topics** from the Visual Basic **Help** menu.

In addition, you can also display the MSDN Library independently by choosing **Programs, MSDN Library 6.0** from the Windows **Start** menu. When the MSDN Library is accessed, you are presented with a Windows Explorer-style display as shown in Figure 21.4.

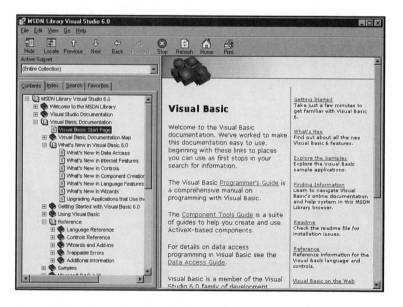

FIGURE 21.4   Accessing Visual Basic Help from the MSDN Library.

Along with the MSDN Library that is installed on your computer with Visual Basic, you also have access to the MSDN Library Online. The MSDN Library is updated every three months and can be accessed on the Web via the MSDN Online Membership. MSDN is a free program that offers access to the MSDN Library Online, a subscription to MSDN Flash, third-party trial downloads, and many other benefits. Registration is quick and easy at `http://msdn.microsoft.com/developer/default.htm` (see Figure 21.5).

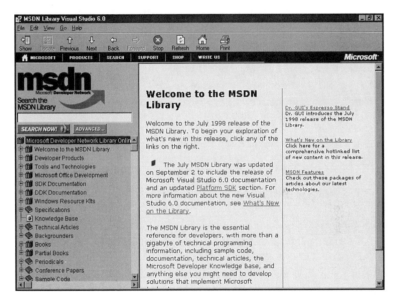

Figure 21.5   Accessing MSDN Online on the Web.

Locating Information in the MSDN Library

There are several different methods that you can use to find the information you need, and many ways to combine these methods so that your search is quick and efficient. The following are the options in the Navigation pane of the MSDN viewer:

- Table of Contents—The **Contents** tab shows you the topics by title. The Table of Contents is an expandable list of everything that is available in the MSDN Library.

- Keyword Index—The **Index** tab displays a list of indexed entries. You can either type a word or scroll through the list.

- Full-Text Search—The **Search** tab is used to locate every occurrence of a word or phrase that might contain a topic.

- Favorites—The **Favorites** tab enables you to create and access a list of the topics that you use most often.

ACCESSING THE VISUAL BASIC WEB SITE

Besides the MSDN Library, as a registered user of Visual Basic you have access to the Microsoft Visual Basic Web site at `http://msdn.microsoft.com /vbasic/`. This site (see Figure 21.6) contains the following:

- Press releases about Visual Basic

- Documentation that is not included with the product

- Samples of Visual Basic code

- Product updates

- Additional tools that can be used with Visual Basic

When you browse the Visual Basic Web site for the first time, make sure you have the product ID for your copy of Visual Basic. This will be required when you register on the Web site. By registering, you will have access to many program upgrades and samples that are available only to a registered user.

GETTING TECHNICAL SUPPORT

Finally, when all else fails, you can open a support call with Microsoft by using the Microsoft Technical Support Web site at `http://www.microsoft.com/support` (see Figure 21.7). Again, you will need the Visual Basic product ID to be able to use this method to obtain technical support.

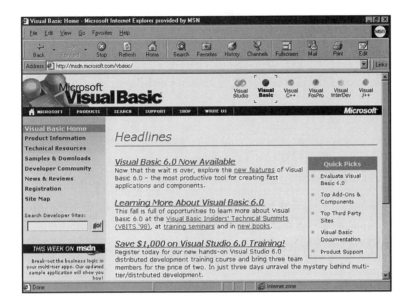

FIGURE 21.6   Accessing the Visual Basic Web site.

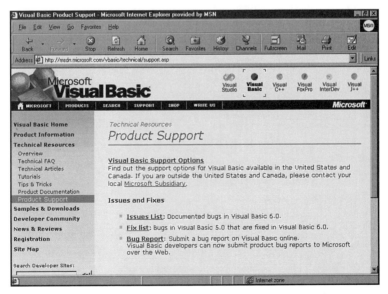

FIGURE 21.7   Getting support from Microsoft over the Web.

After you have started a support call with Microsoft, the technical support representative will correspond with you using email. This method of obtaining support is the best way to get help without waiting on the phone.

SUMMARY

In this lesson, you learned several different ways to get help for Visual Basic. The first and easiest way is by using the features that are included directly in the Visual Basic product. Along with these features, you also have access to a very comprehensive help system with the MSDN libraries installed with Visual Basic. Then, if you still need help, you can communicate with the Visual Basic support group using the Online Support Request Web site.

INDEX

W-Z